An Introduction to the Study of

William Blake

The Reunion of the Soul and the Body

(Frontispiece)

An Introduction to the Study of

William Blake

Max Plowman

ATLANTIC

PUBLISHERS & DISTRIBUTORS (P) LTD

Published by

ATLANTIC

PUBLISHERS & DISTRIBUTORS (P) LTD

7/22, Ansari Road, Darya Ganj, New Delhi-110002
Phones : +91-11-40775252, 40775214, 23273880, 23275880
Fax: +91-11-23285873
Web: www.atlanticbooks.com
E-mail: orders@atlanticbooks.com

Printed & bound in India by Atlantic Print Services

Preface

In the following essays I have tried to indicate certain ways of approach to the poetry of William Blake, in the hope that those who have some appreciation of that poetry, but only limited opportunities for close study of it, may be encouraged to follow their inclination still further. Many who enjoy the *Songs of Innocence and Experience* are discouraged when they come to the so-called Prophetic Books because, quite pardonably, they do not know the way to read Blake. They are distracted by his symbolism and disturbed by his want of logic. They puzzle their brains for a while and then give up. It is all too obviously mystifying.

When first I began to read Blake seriously I thought a complete glossary of his symbols and a *précis* of his myths must be essential. So I bought the Quaritch edition and on a memorable holiday began reading with a friend the exposition of Mr. Ellis. We had not gone far before the sound of the reader's voice and the expression on the hearer's face made imperative the question, "Understandest thou what thou readest?" And the answer being in the negative, we laughingly dropped the weighty volumes (two of Ellis and one of Blake) and went for a bathe. Such treatment was criminally unfair to Blake and not wholly just to Mr. Ellis; but we were young, and Blake is strong meat for babes. Still, I fancy the incident must be typical, because many another must have felt that however long Art may be, Life is short, and a poet who stands in need of all that explanation has only himself to blame if he waits to all eternity for readers.

We come to that conclusion whenever we regard Blake as an intellectual problem. He is not that. He is something very different: much more subtle, much more delicate, much more worthwhile.

Blake is like music. Musical instruments with the same vibrations are, I believe, capable of responding to one another: a note sounded on one will call forth a spontaneous response from another tuned to the same pitch. The poetry of Blake is analogous. The reader must be in tune: in tune to some extent with Blake, but still more in tune with himself. He must be imaginatively awake, intellectually keen and frankly wholehearted. If not, he will usually hear nothing but the most terrible dissonance. Moreover, he must be ready to give his ordinary critical faculty a good rest. While we are on the road to the understanding of Blake, it is useless to read him critically. Above all, we must not expect to find the music on any kind of annotated programme. We must listen, intently and patiently and not be too readily discouraged by inharmonious sounds but wait until we hear a phrase that deeply pleases us. When we hear it, we do well to remember it, for that phrase is probably our clue to the whole symphony. Yet having found a response, we must not be misled into thinking that mere intellectual effort will now bring all the remaining dissonance into harmony. It will not. Such frantic efforts frustrate themselves, as Mr. Ellis's heroic work very often shows. We must continue to be harmonious, patient, susceptible, and responsive; for Blake's poetry is a spiritual harmony, to be enjoyed and understood according to the measure in which the reader is himself spiritually harmonious.

To say this is not to decry the excellent work of exposition that has already been done, especially by such a keen student of Blake's sources of inspiration as Mr. Foster Damon. To our present immature comprehension of Blake, such work is invaluable, and I gladly take the opportunity of acknowledging my especial indebtedness to this transatlantic friend who has done more than anyone to open up Blake's labyrinths. To his book these essays are as a mere footnote. But Mr. Damon would be the first to agree that since Blake's appeal is primarily and finally a direct one, all that is of real value in Blake can only be obtained by the individual through the exercise of his own imagination in direct contact with Blake's written words. Blake described his work as vision, and vision can only be seen by individual imagination: it cannot be seen through the eyes of another, nor by the aid of the most powerful microscope or telescope of encyclopaedic commentary.

Thus I regard the portions of this book which attempt exposition as the least satisfactory. I have been sedulous to avoid the repetition of other people's discoveries, but I would beg the reader not to allow any interpretation of mine to stand between him and his own unaided pleasure. The desire to share that pleasure he will, I hope, find imperative; but it is a pleasure that can hardly be transferred. At any rate, only by subtler means than those at my command can the delight be transmitted which comes when the apparent veils fall away, and the poet's vision becomes clear. All I hope to have done is to have indicated the way in which this is most likely to happen.

Every book is in some degree the record of an adventure. Objectively, the degree is small in the case of ten short and rather laboured essays. Nevertheless, subjectively they stand for an adventure that is unique in any lifetime. That is perhaps a personal confession; but as the discerning reader cannot fail to notice a progression, I would ask him to remember the adventure of John Bunyan's pilgrim. Then, if he will read the essays in the order they were written, he will, I hope, find even here, similar steps upon the same journey.

List of Illustrations

The Illustration to Milton's "L'Allegro" is taken from a water-colour drawing in the possession of Mr. Adrian Van Sinderen and is reproduced with his kind permission. A similar reproduction first appeared in the None such Edition of Milton's Poems, edited by Mr. Geoffrey Keynes, 1926.

Contents

1

Corporeal Understanding

Some years ago, about the time when my old nurse was beginning to think less highly of herself than she ought to have thought, because she could neither read nor write, I remember that a grave and very learned member of the English nobility set himself the arduous task of deciding which were the hundred best books. Whether he succeeded to his satisfaction or not I do not know, but in due time The Hundred Best Books were published. It became my ambition to acquire them so that I might at least possess foundations for an educated mind, but this ambition went the way of many another, and now I do not even remember the names of the hundred best books. I recall them only to wonder whether they included The Works of William Blake.

I am afraid they didn't; and for my part, just at this moment, I confess to a frame of mind in which, were I offered the ninety and nine or the one that had gone astray, I should prefer the sheep that was lost and read Blake even in preference to the Koran. Such is human perversity, and such the injustice done to those who, in Francis Thompson's phrase, "kept indomitably planting in the defile of fame the established canons."

Within the past hundred years critic after critic has arisen, pulled himself vigorously together and determined that the niche to be occupied by Blake should once for all be definitely decided upon, and that the label the critic affixed, usually on one of the more inaccessible shelves, was *the* place for Blake—let those who had a tincture of Blake's madness say what they liked. And yet, year by year, larger and more important-looking labels are stuck on lower and more accessible shelves, until the day seems to be not far distant when the literary dispenser's apologies will be unnecessary and the complete Blake will be no longer regarded as a narcotic for numskulls but will stare every university undergraduate full in the face.

To the academic eye, things must begin to look ominous when "Jerusalem" is sung in Canterbury Cathedral; for a straw shows which way the wind blows, and Blake among popular song-writers is a portent, more especially when this song is one of personal triumph over academic traditions. Is Blake also among the prophets?

The paradoxical thing about Blake is that he is not. A prophet confessed, with his own intelligible definition of what constituted that functionary, he is not "among" any. He remains, as he lived, alone. And therein lays the secret of the reason why his work has been such a persistent nuisance to orderly criticism. Blake dared to be a Daniel with the same consequence as befell the earlier prophet. He was cast into the lions' den and forgotten—for forty years quite forgotten. But Blake knew all about lions and tigers: he was on such intimate terms with them he gave them human features. So the lions of oblivion and tigers of wrath lay down with him and slept. And now, when the morning breaks, Blake steps out of the lions' den renewed with sleep, and the lions have made such a meal of his detractors that in very fear of them, we of this day begin to write false praise.

Blake cannot be classed. He was the most independent artist that ever lived. He had his own sources of inspiration (so peculiar and strange that no one else has dared to drink from them), his own strange technique, his own method of printing, his own method of illustrating, and his own secret way of reproducing his illustrations. He did everything for himself—including lighting his own fire and fetching his own beer. Little wonder, then, that his work is strange and seems to possess individuality in unique degree, and less wonder that it fails to conform to accepted ideas of what it could, would, might, or should have been.

The significance of this is lost upon us if we imagine that Blake had any desire for singularity, or if we fail to see that he often took pains to conform in all inessential matters with the accepted customs of his day. To him it was a persistent cause for wonder and dismay that friends and acquaintances should so misunderstand his work as to think it willfully odd. Yet with giant courage and saintly humility he gradually overcame the resentment which ostracism begot, and thus was enabled to exhibit his genius at its highest at a time when his work had no public estimation at all and he himself was put down as an eccentric. But be himself he would. "He was one of the few," wrote Samuel Palmer, who knew Blake well, "who are not, in some way or other, double-minded and inconsistent with themselves." Therefore he stands, a human landmark of faith—not mere faith in himself, but faith in life's purpose for those who are "not disobedient to the heavenly vision." Blake is the chief example in English literature of implicit obedience to a good conscience. He never trimmed, never pot-boiled, and never dallied: above all, he never doubted his own inspiration. Thus his fidelity to purpose made him unique: a figure unmistakable that has become for us the prototype of the individual artist.

Blake cannot be classed. You may say that he was the first of the great 19th century poets: a badly educated mystic who derived his mysticism from Paracelsus and Jacob Boehme: an artist whose sense of movement occasionally triumphed over the bad, elongated, sculpturesque tradition of his day; but when you have said that you have said nothing about the essential Blake, nothing which anyone who has felt the delight Blake is capable of creating will recognize as indicative of it.

Similarly he cannot be estimated. The comparative standards give way before one who does not compete. He said of Wordsworth, "I cannot think that real poets have any competition. None are greatest in the Kingdom of God. It is so in Poetry." And in truth so it is. Poetry is the revelation of truth as perceived by the individual soul. It is either a real expression of that perception, or a false pretence to perception. If it is real it is poetry, unique in value as the human soul that gives it birth. If it is false it is worthless. What is true is different in kind from what is false. You cannot compare them, and poetry that is real is, and always must be, unique, and therefore essentially incomparable.

Blake's practice makes this clear. Judged by those barren objective standards which have done such dismal duty since the time of Matthew Arnold, I know of only one of Blake's lyrics that can be deemed perfect, and it is significant that the poem is Blake's lament over the traditional muses. When he had written that poem and a few more in the same manner, he bade an everlasting farewell to formalism, and henceforward put his trust in the living image which begot in him the desire to create, Knowing that if he was faithful to vision the image would make for itself the only body it had a right to live in.[1] By so doing, he not only killed the formalism of the 18th century but, before it was born, signed the death-warrant of all the pretentious exhibitionism that has been written since.

So try him which way we will, the category business fails. It fails, not because of Blake's excellence, but because of his difference. He was not a producer of literature, a painter of charming pictures, an amiable social figure; he did not consider art an elegant flourish to the signature of opulence: he was a man who believed that poetry was the power of transmitting divine communications: an artist who believed that "art can never exist without Naked (*i.e.* spiritual) Beauty displayed": a man of titanic energy, gentle as a child, who was always ready to speak the truth. The only answer we can give to the question, where does Blake stand? Must be, Upon his own feet.

Another interesting reason why Blake cannot be duly labeled and pigeon-holed, after the labour-saving manner of literary criticism, is that while everybody understands some part, nobody understands the whole of his work. Personally I doubt if anyone ever will, just as I doubt whether any one human being can have complete knowledge and understanding of the soul of another. But we must know precisely what we are doing before we lay blame at Blake's door on this account. Blake strove to portray the soul of man. In so doing, of course, he portrayed his own soul. But the soul (your soul and mine as well as Blake's) has depths and heights which are beyond the range of purely intellectual concepts. The body can be seen, measured, anatomized, analysed; but, despite the painful efforts of psychoanalysis, the soul is beyond such survey: it must be spiritually sensed; and he who intends faithfully to portray that which has only infinite bounds, must be prepared to see his lines extending beyond the range of human knowledge into those

1. For a perfect example of this compare the two stanzas from the Rossetti MS. beginning, "I laid me down upon a bank."

realms where apprehension supplants intelligence. It is not to be thought that the limited understanding which suffices for things material is going to make a total comprehension of that which is confessedly beyond the range of matter.

Whether Blake's attempt to portray the human soul was wise or an artistic impossibility is another question; but granted that his desire was to bring the soul of man objectively into conscious view, then the fact that the image portrayed has elements in it so strange as to be unrecognizable, or that it at sometimes appears to be no image at all, but looks like a crystal scratched with hieroglyphics, while at others it grows, intensifies, colours and pervades like light at sunrise, and again at others is like the sudden raising of a blind, letting sunlight into a new chamber in the house of life—that these strange and seemingly uncontrollable contrasts of blank misgiving and vivid illumination should always be happening to the reader, is not after all much to be wondered at when we remember what it is we are contemplating.

Of course, to suggest that what one man wrote may never be wholly comprehended by any one other is to the privet-hedge mind the very apology of madness for madness; but to those of freer growth it will occur that in degree this applies to any profound writer and his reader, and is true in the exact measure to which the writer attempts to survey the heights and plumb the depths of the soul. It is only peculiarly true of Blake because honest writer about Blake has been faced with the alternatives of keeping silence until understanding was complete, or making an open confession of ignorance. Of course, there is a third way out of the difficulty, which more professional scribes have not been slow to take, and that is to assume the comparative worthlessness of what has not been understood and to assure the inquiring reader that he will only waste his time if he goes mining for other ore than has already been brought to the surface. This course, if taken with an air of omniscience, is temporarily very effective: but it is apt to look silly when a new adventurer reclaims more metal.

However, facing this ignorance honestly, what is to be done? Superficially one would say, explore the whole ground and then write. But the problem is peculiar and not to be solved so easily. Blake did not appeal primarily to the reasoning faculty. "The most sublime Poetry" he describes as "allegory addressed to the intellectual powers, while it is altogether hidden from the corporeal understanding." Poetry that does these inverses common practice. Most poets appeal primarily to "the corporeal understanding" trusting that through it they may find a way to the "intellectual powers." And when criticism deals with such poets it can always pass muster on the safe ground he strove to do what had never been done before: to portray the soul, not subjectively through the images of nature, but objectively through the images of his own imagination. Whether any one person will ever comprehend all the images of Blake's imagination seems doubtful, but that he offers to every intelligent reader a little universe of images which seem to be the immediate personal gift of the poet is not doubtful, but the continuous experience of every sympathetic student. Equally certain it is that one-tenth of the treasure thus received would be full amends for those vacant hours when the understanding sleeps and Blake is like a forest of undergrowth.

The extraordinary pleasure derived from reading Blake, or seeing into his pictures, has been the mainspring of every book written about him that is worth reading. But every writer—Gilchrist, Swinburne, Yeats, Ellis, Russell, Raleigh, Berger, Bin yon, Wick steed, Damon, Figgie and others that I have read—has been confronted with the same perplexity in greater or less degree. Each has experienced a delight in Blake which demanded some kind of expression, but each has been faced with the fact that his understanding of Blake was only partial. Literary criticism as a fine art naturally demands a unity. It is impossible to achieve objective unity if the subject is partially unknown. Hence, without doubt, every of "corporeal understanding" when it fails to soar with the poet on the wings of the "intellectual powers." But Blake offers no such safeguard to dignity. He cuts the ground from under our feet, and we are either with him in his flight, or on our way to the abyss.

The snag lies in that "complete understanding." I have already said that I doubt whether it will ever be achieved by a single mind; and now I would add that I doubt whether its achievement, if possible, would be desirable, or even in accord with Blake's intention. This sounds rather like sour grapes; so I hasten to confess that I will entertain at considerable expense any writer who holds a contrary opinion and can be as good as his word. But Blake's manner of address to us being different from that commonly employed, we may reasonably assume that our method of approach must be different. "Complete understanding" of any great poet is, of course, a misuse of words. We understand according to the measure of our "intellectual powers." But when the address is superficially to our corporeal understandings, no great hiatus is caused by our acceptance of the superficial meaning for the profound. We can pass cheerfully over a passage like:

> Pity like a naked new-born babe
> Striding the blast,

to more reasonable matter. But when in Blake we read:

> Tell them to obey their Humanities and not pretend Holiness
> When they are murderers as far as my Hammer and Anvil permit,

the corporeal mind pulls up at "murderers" with a jolt, unless the intellectual powers are busily at work prompting us to the consciousness of the allegorical meaning of that Hammer and Anvil. Before we can attain to understanding of any kind, we must be aware of an implicit meaning, in this case suggested by other lines of the same poem which tell us that

> The blow of his Hammer is Justice, the swing of his Hammer Mercy,
> The force of Loss's Hammer is eternal Forgiveness.

The example, however, is a poor one because it suggests that Blake might be completely understood by a nimble use of cross-references, which is very far from being the case. The use of Blake as cross-word puzzle is unprofitable.

The point is, that while "complete understanding" remains our goal, were it capable of being achieved logically, Blake would be like a worked-out mine, or like that perfect day of the popular song. We should have come to an end. There is no such end to poetry, even though it is poetry which seems to disguise itself with strange names that have precise but hidden meanings—names that tease the corporeal mind into the belief that a knowledge of the allegory would yield us "complete understanding." It is not so. The intellectual powers alone hold the true meaning, and that meaning partakes of the nature of infinity. It is poetry, and poetry is universal truth seen in minute identity, an image of the eternal which finally has no "meaning" being irradiant with all meaning by being itself.

Thus Time, with its accustomed inevitability, has turned the whirligig, and finely avenged William Blake of the charge made by criticism that he was mad. For half a century now criticism has been compelled to go on hands and knees before his work, begging precisely that gift which madness is deficient of, at the same time being obliged before an open-mouthed audience, either to confess its want of intellectual power, or to disguise its ignorance in a pretentious wisdom that is almost hourly made to eat its own words. Which spectacle is itself an allegory of the wisdom of this world and its foolishness in the face of higher wisdom?

2

The Imaginative Image

At the conclusion of the well-known passage in which Blake describes his vision of the rising sun, he says:

"I question not my corporeal or vegetative eye any more than I would question a window concerning a sight. I look thro' it and not with it."

Blake's own work should be regarded in a similar way. To the sterile mind and the roving eye it yields almost nothing beside defects. When the most magnificent of Blake's designs to Blair's *Grave* was first published, the art critic, I think of *The Examiner*, could only see in the rapturous meeting of Body and Soul a female figure apparently diving into the mouth of a male one; and though no doubt his corporeal sight was good, such a critic would need to have scales removed from his eyes before he was really capable of seeing what Blake drew.

It is the same in reading Blake. To the dull, unimaginative mind such a simple and sublime poem as *Little Lamb, who made thee?* Is almost idiotic. Literally speaking, no child in its senses would think of addressing such a question to a beast of the field, for the youngest child knows that the only articulate reply to the lamb could make would be "Baa." So that we have not very far to go in our reading of Blake before we find that the literal use of words which suffices for newspaper and novel reading breaks down altogether, and Blake is a sealed book to us unless we are prepared for a finer use of words.

Blake drew and wrote to reveal spiritual truth. Spiritual truth does not lie on the surface of appearances: indeed, it is often contradicted by appearances, and where Blake found that contradiction he did not scruple to sacrifice the apparent fact for the unapparent truth. No physical body rises from a recumbent position as the female figure rises in another of those illustrations to Blair's *Grave,* "The Soul hovering over the Body reluctantly parting from Life." Yet adherence to the physical fact of gravitation would not have permitted Blake to express his conception, and this obvious defiance of natural law has made that expression magnificently possible. When the less gives way to the greater, beauty always results, unless there is doubt in the mind of the creator, and then, of course, the less has not truly given way: there is conflict, and doubt produces falsehood.

The Soul Hovering over the Body Reluctantly Parting from Life

A passage from the explanatory comments Blake made in his manuscript book upon his picture representing *The Last Judgment*, gives us, I think, a clear indication of how Blake would have liked us to regard his work. It runs: "the Imaginative Image returns by the seed of Contemplative Thought." The sentence is reminiscent of Keats's famous letter to Reynolds in which he describes how "anyone grand and spiritual passage serves as a starting-post towards all 'the two and thirty Palaces,' " and concludes with the sage advice: "let us open our leaves like a flower and be passive and receptive, budding patiently under the eye of Apollo and taking hints from every noble insect that favours us with a visit."

"The Imaginative Image returns by the seed of Contemplative Thought." That was Blake's description of the activity of creation. Inversely, those who read him most profitably read him for the return of the imaginative image which he held in his mind's eye while he wrote. It was to create that image that he put pen to paper, and Blake's counsel is that we should recreate the same image through the fructification of the seed of contemplative thought. It is useless to wrestle with Blake. We all do it, but it is quite useless. No amount of learning, Blake-lore or other, will of itself yield us the imaginative image which is the only thing worth having from Blake. It is equally useless to behave like young fledglings in the nest, and open wide and empty mouths in the hope that something luscious may drop in. The mind, like the man in the Gospel at the pool of Bethesda, must be ready for the moving of the water, awake, observant, indifferent to mere reasonable probability, and, above all, full of that imagination which is synthetic.

To understand and appreciate an artist we must first find out what he is trying to do. It is waste of time to go to the butcher or baker for the works of the candlestick-maker. It is futile to go to Shakespeare for the kind of pleasure we derive from Mr. Bernard Shaw; and it is equally misguided to go to Blake expecting that a reasonable interpretation of his words will suffice. That it will not, is clear to any simple-minded reader, apart from the mass of literature about Blake which has been written from the purely reasonable standpoint. Naturalistic art was Blake's abhorrence: the mere representation of natural objects he held in contempt.

Spiritual truth was his aim, and so far was he from regarding imaginative and naturalistic painting as the same thing, that he described what he once called Historical Designing and Portrait Painting as different arts, "as distinct as any two arts can be."

"If the fool would persist in his folly he would become wise." Blake never understood what we may call representational art. He could not see that without departing from stark natural semblance it was possible for an artist to express profound spiritual truth. But his blindness to this fact was due to excess of light. If Blake had ever come to appreciate the inherent merits of portrait painting, his true genius would have been sidetracked. What Blake's good angel had in store for him was the power to demonstrate that imagination could overleap natural resemblance and arrive at spiritual truth without the pedestrian steps which most of the artists of his day-thought all important. And in so doing, Blake helped to define forever what is essential and what inessential to art. For just as in poetry Blake's abandonment of formalism and implicit trust in the living image tolled the knell of that kind of verse which is a bad substitute for a pleasant walk in the country, so Blake's persistent resolve to paint nothing but his own visions lifted the art of painting forever out of the ruck of mere representation.

The effect of his practice in both arts has been tremendous. It has been said that Blake was an Ishmaelite who left no disciples and founded no school. But apart altogether from the little coterie of copyists who gathered round him in his declining years, Blake's spiritual disciples have been the most numerous and the most potent forces in art since his day. Blake freed Western art from slavish adherence to Nature. Thousands who enjoy that enfranchisement have hardly heard his name, but all that art which endeavours to express spiritual values by direct methods that employ Nature as a handmaid but scorn her as a mistress, all such art is in the direct line of descent from Blake. It matters little that Blake would not recognize many of his own children, the impetus his faith in what he called visionary art gave to simplification of method has lasted a century and continues.

On poetry his influence is perhaps even more obvious. Descriptive poetry, which flourished like a bay-tree during Blake's life and lengthened out its complacent existence in all the inferior work of the 19th century, has vanished. It has gone completely. Nowadays, even Mr. Masefield, who might be thought to be of the old line, relies for his effect upon humanistic and dramatic elements in his art which are quite foreign to the kind of poetry that relied for its appeal upon its power of reviving amiable memories, or of transferring the reader mentally to scenes of natural beauty. Poetry as rhyming journalism is a thing of the past. Even poetry as a criticism of life no longer holds sway, but the trend of modern poetry is in the direction first pointed by Blake's *Songs of Innocence and Experience*, towards the creation of images. Modern poetry endeavours, by suggestion, by implication, to create a reverie in which mental images are presented. The prevailing style favours an economy of words and simplicity of manner that is derived straight from Blake's earlier poems.

That Blake, despite his immense influence should not have been better understood would be singular, were it not for the fact that we seldom understand the forces which most impress us. Apart from all question of the prophetic element in poetry, great poets have always been far more conscious of the derivative than of the original elements in their work. This is not to deny them consciousness of power; that consciousness has been common to them all, not excepting Keats. But originality implies singularity, and whenever a poet recognizes singularity in himself it is with dismay, as Blake illustrated with humorous pathos when he wrote,

> Oh, why was I born with a different face!

And when a poet happens to be both greatly original and obviously singular, and when he happens moreover to have been born into an age which is religiously commonplace and conscientiously prosaic, his case is a hard one; for the insensitive air without, tends in time to shut him in upon himself, and singularity may grow into peculiarity, a peculiarity which will be difficult for any generation to understand.

It is perhaps an idle fancy, but I have sometimes wondered whether the marvelous means by which Blake came to express himself was not due in part to the fact that he had no audience. If a poet can obtain no hearing, and if he happens also to be an artist, why should he not amuse himself by creating a chorus to his song—an echo to its sound—by peopling his manuscript with figures, animate and inanimate, which uphold the argument and take from it its lone reverberations? If, in the beginning, the Word found satisfaction when it became flesh, might not these words— otherwise apparently uncreative—find social satisfaction if they were wedded to lineal images capable of responding to and reinforcing their spoken appeal?

Such an idea is probably the merest moonshine, but however the result came about, what Blake did was both original and singular to such a degree that I doubt whether it has even yet been appreciated. For he did not merely write his poems and add to them decorative designs. He did not even write the poems and add interpretive drawings. But with extraordinary artifice he made poems and designs interdependent; so that a page of his work represents nothing so much as a crystal into which the "reader" gazes until a single image reveals itself, which image is the creation of both poem and design inseparable.

Six years divide Blake's earliest book of poems, *Poetical Sketches*, from the *Songs of Innocence*. Those six years mark the biggest change he ever experienced. In them he passed from the representational to the symbolic poet: from the exquisite traditionalist to the genuine creator: from the youth who re-echoed the loveliest strains in English lyrical poetry to the man who set forth from the Garden of Innocence to trace the course of human life from Eden to the new Jerusalem.

The change is reflected by the manner in which the two books were produced. The *Poetical Sketches* were sponsored by the Reverend Henry Matthew, printed in plain, traditional type, without illustrations, at the expense of others, and the book was designed to be sold in the ordinary way. In contrast to this, everything connected with the *Songs of Innocence* was Blake's own work. He wrote the poems and drew the designs, etched them in an entirely original manner, printed them himself, coloured them with his own hand, and finally published, advertised, and sold them himself. Blake had learnt the mighty lesson of self-reliance.

In those six years he had gone deep. It is as if instead of offering his lyrics like welcome drinks on the highway, he had retired to the forest, where his poems had become limpid pools, now catching the gold of sunbeams, now appearing turquoise as the sky above them, now dark with shadow of giant oaks, and now fretted with the wind that blows where it wills. Seen casually as you hurry along they are charming enough. But stay and ponder over them: look deeply into their depths and you will see strange images of

> The varying clouds, like paradises stretch'd in the expanse,
> With towns and villages and temples, tents, sheep-folds and pastures
> Where dwell the children of the elemental worlds in harmony,

Visions hardly to be suspected in what were, apparently, the simplest lyrics ever written.

There is something of the mediaeval magician about Blake's Manner of presenting his poetry. Beautiful to both ear and eye, this poetry is for the first time the poetry of sight and sound. Each poem is a jewel-casket, beautiful in itself. Open the casket a little way and you are dazzled by the wealth within. Look long and you will see that every jewel has its place, and the casket within and without is itself an image of something yet more beautiful and emits rays of light brighter than the sun at noontide.

"If the spectator could enter into these Images in his Imagination, approaching them on the fiery chariot of his contemplative thought: if he could enter into Noah's Rainbow, or into his bosom, or could make a friend and companion of one of these Images of wonder, which always entreats him to leave mortal things (as he must know), then would he arise from his grave, then would he meet the Lord in the air, and then he would be happy."

The seed of contemplative thought has become a fiery chariot imaginatively reminiscent of Elijah's chariot. Note well the appeal to us to *enter into* these images. This "entering into" is that looking "through the eye, not with it." Blake's poems and pictures are not flat surfaces. Like the landscapes of Cezanne, it is their depth that interests us, and the deeper we look the more the image comes forth. With his usual perception, Mr. Joseph Wick steed suggests this in a passage descriptive of the half-finished designs to Dante's *Divine Comedy*. "To me," he says, "it seems that it must have been somewhat as though Blake sat at his canvas or sheet and gazed *into* it, as a man might gaze *out* of a mist-obscured window. Presently he seems to see through it, and the dim outlines of a scene appear, projected, we may suppose, by the inner light of genius upon the paper. Slowly, as his genius works, the mist seems to clear away and the window less and less to obscure the scene beyond. He traces its details upon the surface, until at last the full clear history has been transcribed on to the sheet and a stainless window opened into the regions of imagination."

In an especial sense it therefore takes two to make any of Blake's poems: one to write and one to read; and the resultant pleasure to the reader will be in exact ratio to the imagination he employs. As these poems were not constructed according to the pattern of reason, they do not invariably yield one single image which is *the* meaning. That meaning fluctuates as the meaning of every poem by every poet varies according to the imagination and experience of the particular reader, only more strikingly in Blake because, like no other, appealing solely to the imaginative faculty, he writes from individual to individual, and not from the individual to the general reasoning faculty of men. He speaks, not to commonsense, but to individual senses. It was waste of time to argue with those who would pretend on this ground that Blake's poems lack determinate form. They have not only form, but forms. Each poem is a prism, and if you see blue while I see violet, pray do not let us destroy the prism in a foolish argument as to the colour it emits.[1]

And more generally speaking, let it not be thought that because Blake used images his thought lacked definition. This is the supposition of those who do not really understand the difference between poetry and prose, and who fancy that the poet uses imagery when he is uncertain in his mind. Poetry is not the poverty but the plenitude of language—the divine over plus of thought which seizes upon correspondences and whilst

1. This has already been done. Drawings of Blake's that offended "corporeal" eyes have been destroyed, as the pages of his *Vala* ruefully declare.

placing them in relation, endows them with the superfluity of the wealth that initially belonged to the principal matter. The images of a poet are not guests at the feast compelled to come in from the highways and hedges. They flock into his mind, they come without bidding, they offer themselves arrayed in the most suitable wedding garments, and the number he cannot entertain is always greater than the number of those who are given a seat at the feast.

Blake was most strict in his door keeping. The wandering guests of fancy occasionally found a place, but far from the chief seats. Those who occupy the important places are worthy of the closest attention. Strange they may appear at first sight; but let us never forget, Blake was the most orderly of hosts.

In the passage we have quoted the relevance of the fiery chariot has been suggested. A casual reader might well fancy that Noah's rainbow and his bosom were mere flights of hyperbole. It is not the ease. Noah's rainbow was the emblem of promise to man that the waters should never again cover the earth. Hence, if I enter Noah's rainbow, I sensibly enjoy the promise that Deified Vengeance is at an end, that the Age of Grace has superseded the Age of Law. More particularly, I am individually and socially made conscious that the flood of materialism which immerses you and me has, in our spiritual worlds, already receded, never again wholly to cover us. Yet further, entering this rainbow, I know, by "spiritual sensation" as distinct from the intellectual transference of ideas, that as the rainbow is caused by the refraction of light in a prism of water and is at once a thing of ineffable beauty and pathetic transience, so this physical body of mine and the whole world of created matter is a refraction of divine unity, evanescent in substance, beautiful in appearance, pathetic in its transience, yet at the same time an emblem of the divine promise. Mortality seen in the light of Eternity is thus transfigured, and this transfiguration I may experience by "entering Noah's rainbow."

Of "his bosom," let it suffice to say that Noah was the friend of God and the saviour of Man. To be the object of the love of such a one is good cause for happiness. Of "the grave" we shall have much to say later.

3

The use of Symbols

The real trouble about Blake is his vocabulary. If a man in his first conversation with you were to say, for example: "There is nothing like death. Death is the best thing that can happen in life; but most people die so late and take such an unmerciful time in dying, God knows, their neighbours never see them rise from the dead"—well, you might reasonably think that he had strained common sense for the sake of paradox. But Blake made many such remarks to Crabbe Robinson in all seriousness, and would by them have conveyed profound truths, only Mr. Robinson was incapable of appreciating what his peculiar friend meant by "death," or many of the other words Blake used with uncommon meanings. When he spoke of Sight, Imagination, Nature, Reason, Genius, and even Love, Heaven or Hell, to men like Flaxman, Hayley or the Reverend Doctor Trusler, he intended to signify things which were, unfortunately, beyond their comprehension. That was partly because they were merely unimaginative; but it was also because Blake gave to such words peculiar and enlarged meaning. When he writes, "Where any view of money exists, art cannot be carried on, but war only, by pretences to the two impossibilities, Chastity and Abstinence, gods of the heathen," one is justified in believing that nothing but a liberal education in Blakean terminology can give to these words their author's meaning.

Here, as always in Blake, face value is small value. Here the so-called scientific use of words is not merely inadequate, as it is with every other poet, it breaks down altogether. We must have an imaginative meaning or a false one.

What writer has not sighed for a new vocabulary? To see the words flowing like the River of Life itself, spotless in purity, crystal in clearness, fresh as Eden—every word exacts in its full meaning, unsullied by use, untainted by custom—it is an enchanting dream full of the most amiable self-granulation. But, after the way of things sighed for, it is never realized by those who sigh. Something very like it is the chief reward obtained by a man of genius at the end of a lifetime's labour. Shakespeare must have enjoyed it in *The Tempest.* Milton does not seem to have been much troubled with the second-hand in *Samson Agonists.* Words had come to obey their wills because they willed so deeply.

The case of Blake is different. Shakespeare and Milton were, in a sense, men of the world. They were men of public influence who had much traffic with affairs and in consequence their language never got far from common currency. But Blake was isolated. Intensification of the poetic vernacular of his day would have been quite useless to him; indeed, his "Lines in Imitation of Pope" show what he thought could be achieved in that direction. But words pregnant with meaning—clean, rarefied words, fresh from the mint of individual thought were essential. So in the day of dearth he sowed his own crop. He gave to some words of everyday use his own specific, intensified meaning, and when he found even this inadequate, he coined words of his own.

But we are on dangerous ground here. It is easy to suggest that Blake wanted to create a new mythology and so spent a pleasant evening selecting a fresh catalogue of names for his gods and goddesses. Any such idea is as false as ludicrous. Blake was first, foremost and always an imaginative writer, and if we leave imagination out of account in any consideration of him, we are on the high road to self-imposed misunderstanding.

Just how and when his common vocabulary seemed to him inadequate we shall probably never know; but it is interesting to speculate upon the reasons that led him to take the plunge into the use of symbols.

Take the case of Urizen. Blake had spent much time before he came to the writing of *The Marriage of Heaven and Hell* in trying to define that mental power which circumscribed the mind of man. He had conceived of a universal Poetic Genius as the source of being—a power which, while it permeated all life, might yet be described as "the true Man." To balance this conception, he needed a contrary principle to express the obvious limitation which this power suffers; and at first he seems to have been content to call it "Reason." In *The Marriage of Heaven and Hell* Reason and Desire are the contrasted powers; but it appears to me that before he reached the conclusion of his great manifesto, the absence of precise correspondence with his thought which the word Reason conveyed, and the extraneous connotations it inevitably called up, had begun to impress him; so that when he leaves the pedestrian road of prose and finds his native freedom in *A Song of Liberty* (which is, without doubt, an integral part of *The Marriage of Heaven and Hell),* a personification appears, later identified as Urizen, simply to give more precise definition to the principle of life which is eternal limitation.

Blake thought with an exactitude hard to follow. The circle beyond which most people's thought becomes hazy and indefinite is not very large. But with Blake it is immense—far wider than Milton and comparable only with Dante. It is not merely that he thought in what are sometimes called cosmic terms, the distinctive feature of Blake's thought is its distinctness. He sustained the power of delineation and definition far beyond where we are commonly content to generalize, and it was because he was working quite definitely in regions of the human soul hitherto untraversed with chart and map that Blake required new names and did not scruple to make them as and when the need occurred.

The first use of names that can by a stretch be called symbolic occurred in 1787. Blake was then thirty years of age and to amuse himself and express his contempt for the literary tea-party, he began writing a social squib called *An Island in the Moon.* It never got beyond a few pages and was obviously tossed off to give vent to a mood. Grave-browed gentlemen, possibly fresh from their own literary tea-parties, have found in it signs of mental instability, vulgarity and want of taste. Others have thought it highly amusing and only wished that Blake had found time to finish what would have been an older companion to *Alice in Wonderland.* The inanities of literary gossip, the futile inconsequence of drawing-room conversation, and the pretentiousness of specialized learning in its shirt-sleeves have never been better hit off. And it is here that Blake began to use descriptive names expressive of the particular vocations of his characters. Steelyard, Suction, Quid, Sip sop, Mrs. Gimblet, Mrs. Nannicanti-pot and Miss Gittipin are really Blake's first essays in symbolism.

An Island in the Moon also contains the first draft of three poems belonging to the *Songs of Innocence:* "Holy Thursday," "Nurse's Song," and "The Little Boy Lost." Again those who do not understand the scope and freedom of an original mind have gaped with wonder that the dew of the morning should be found on muddy earth. The real wonder is not that these poems should first appear here, but that they should have appeared anywhere.

Blake was thirty years of age when he began to write the *Songs of Innocence.* This seems to me the astounding fact; for the *Songs of Innocence* express for the first time in English literature the spontaneous happiness of childhood. Now nothing in the whole world of emotion is of lighter texture than the happiness of a child. Like the dew, it vanishes with the first rays of the sun, and its essential quality, spontaneity, is a thing never to be recalled. One would have thought that to write songs which not only have this quality but are so deeply dyed in it that they are its expression, the singer must have been one who carried over into his manhood all his childish innocence. But Blake was thirty: he had been married five years and was working hard to earn a livelihood.

The spontaneity of these songs is the spontaneity of art, not of nature, of imagination and not of experience. Nothing but the purest imagination could give so stainless an image. The spontaneity of a child is so elusive it escapes the faintest touch of self-consciousness and, but for Blake, might never have been brought into the realm of art. Its pure expression has never been made before or since. Compare the *Songs of Innocence* with Stevenson's *Child's Garden of Verses*, and we are at once conscious of an immense difference. Stevenson writes of his own childhood, making the reminiscent efforts and fanciful condescension of a grown man. Blake recaptures the child mind. He gathers the flower with the dew upon it. He does not merely write about childish happiness; he becomes the happy child. He does not speak of, or for, the child; he lets the child speak its own delight and, what is most marvelous, there are no false tones in his voice. Stevenson is particular: he writes memoirs of his own childhood: he expresses what he remembers of his own wonder or fancy, his childish hopes and fears. Blake is universal; he expresses the natural delight in life of every happy child in the world. The cry of his "Little Boy Lost" is the cry of every child at the first discovery of loneliness.

All this is admitted, but what is not so widely recognized is the fact that these songs are all symbolic. "The Lamb" is a symbol of "the Lamb of God that takes away the sin of the world." "The Echoing Green" is not only the record of a happy day; it is a symbolic presentation of the Day of Innocence from sunrise to sunset. "Infant Joy," "The Little Black Boy," and the "Laughing Song," symbolize the three ages of Innocence: Infancy, Childhood, and Youth. "A Cradle Song," "Nurse's Song," and "Holy Thursday" are symbolic of the same three ages of man, this time in relation to society; and the remaining poems, which image the human soul in its quest of self-realization, are all of even deeper symbolic import. Reading them in the order Blake once decided they should be placed, we pass through consecutive stages of growth from infancy to self-consciousness.

This makes the case difficult for those who say they can do with Blake except when he is symbolic. It shuts them off to the *Poetical Sketches* which, beautiful as they are, are admittedly prentice work. It is a mistake to say that the symbolism of the *Songs of Innocence* is so unobtrusive that it can well be neglected. Without that symbolism the songs could not have been written, and unawareness of the cause of delight is by no means the finest way of appreciation.

The truth is that all poetry is symbolic in degree. When Shakespeare writes "and Phoebus 'gins arise," and we know Phoebus as a symbol of the sun, our pleasure is all the greater because the poet's use of a figure (which has no actual or naturalistic resemblance to the sun, but is yet fraught with poetic imagery of the sun) overrides our naturalistic objections and seizes upon a higher perception of the truth. Blake does the same thing with the lamb, and by studying how he came to use the figure of the lamb symbolically we shall see how he began to use symbols and how they grew, as it were, under his hand.

Blake was a religious man. At the time he was writing these songs he was a member of the Swedenborgian Church.

He could not, therefore, write about a lamb without stirring in his imagination all the connotations of that word. Agnus Dei was more real to him than any woolly beast of the field, so the double image (or what Blake afterwards called "a two-fold vision") appears, to the infinite enrichment of the poem. Blake's thought was deepening rapidly all the while he was writing these *Songs of Innocence* and gradually he came to realize—if, indeed, he had not already done so before he began—that poetry of the naturalistic order, which he could write so well, as the *Poetical Sketches* testify, was only indirectly capable of carrying his freight: that the naturalistic method impeded the spiritual intent: that words so used had not the depth of meaning he wished to give his words. Therefore, when he writes "Little Lamb, God bless thee," he carries the mind beyond the creature in the fields to the young and innocent child whom he identifies with the Lamb of God, and the harmony of those three concurring images—the lamb, the child, and the Saviour of the World—all images of Innocence—is the true cause of our delight in the poem.

Blake's theme was the soul of man. From the *Songs of Innocence* to *The Ghost of Abel*, his aim was to reveal the nature of the soul. This is ultimately the concern of every true poet. Blake differs from others in that it was his whole concern. For him the soul of man was the epitome of all things. Not only did he see all things reflected in it, but he believed the soul to be the dynamic life of the world, and the world itself to be a reflection, or shadow, of the reality which had its true existence in the soul.

He believed that all things existed in Eternity— not that they were born in Time with a faint hope of extending Time to an everlasting futurity. All things had eternal existence, and their manifestation in Time was a subjective sensory impression. Human life was, as it were, the middle C of a piano whose bass and treble notes extended both ways to infinity, and what he desired to do was to restore to the minds of men the continuous consciousness of infinity which he believed rationalism—or the tyranny of the reasoning over the poetic faculty—had largely obliterated. He desired to do this because he believed that this world and all its happenings could only be seen in true proportion if they were regarded as projections of the spiritual world. He spoke of "seeing the Eternal which is always present to the wise"; and said that "if the doors of perception were cleansed, everything would appear to man as it is, infinite."

Blake's aim being clear to him, how was he to attain it? Symbols, as Dr. Freud has shown, are the only language of the soul. When Blake realized exactly what he wanted to write about, what other means than symbols could he employ? How else could the immaterial adventures of the soul find sensible means of expression?

The pendulum of human thought swings perpetually between the conception of this world as the be-all and end-all of life, and the idea that material existence is of no importance. Poised between two eternities, neither bound to the earth like the worm, nor free of the heavens like the eagle, man stands with his feet on the ground and his head in the air, the very image of all that is indeterminate. Today he is Johnny-head-in-air and has his eyes so fixed upon the whither that he cannot see the ground beneath his feet. Tomorrow he is Bunyan's Man with the Muck-Rake, so obsessed with the evils that surround him that he cannot see the crown of glory above his head. On Sunday he is sure that a true conception of the transcendent God will proportionate all human life. On Monday he is equally certain that an incarnate Deity is the only true conception.

Literature, the expression of human thought, is conditioned by the fashionable vagaries that beset the thought of its time. The fashionable literature of Blake's day was naturally concerned with order, because the thought of those times was concentrated upon the maintenance of order. If ever there was an age of the muck-rake it was surely the end of the 18th century. Blake was the revolutionary prophet who pointed to the crown above man's head.

The fashionable literature of our day is concerned with the analysis of society, because we live in a scientific era which is concerned with the analysis of the material world. Hence, we live on a kind of Monday: transcendence is out of fashion (or was until very recently: one can hardly say, the fashions change so soon). We say proudly that we are concerned with life, which we do know, and not with death which we do not know—or, at least, only with material death which can be analysed.

> Into the breast that gives the rose
> Shall I with shuddering fall?

We still echo Meredith's failing to realize that while the physical body answers No, the response of consciousness is a loud and terror-struck Yes. Since Darwin, life has been ordered in relation to the body rather than the soul of man: the soul has, so to speak, had to take a back seat in view of its hypothetical nature and our new-found knowledge of the body. We do not say body and soul: we say science and religion, but it is all the same.

Fashion must go its own way; but philosophy, which the dictionary tells us deals with ultimate reality, must take cognizance of something besides matter. It must, of course, include consciousness. Hence, no philosophy can be regarded as a philosophy of life which is not also a philosophy of death, for man has very-definite consciousness in regard to death. The conception of life as a gay adventure between two precipices has never yet satisfied a reasonable mind. From the day human consciousness begins it must have some attitude toward infinity, for infinity is our nearest neighbour, and not to be conscious of what surrounds us is surely the essence of unreason?

In literature the consciousness of infinity is betokened by a sense of the sublime. One almost instinctively apologizes for the use of a word so terribly out of fashion. Who cares for this unknown quantity today? What poems are written in the hope of achieving it? What dramas convey its atmosphere? Dear me, no! We are too well aware of what lies in closest proximity to the sublime to be taking any risks of that kind. Yet art cannot be created without taking risks and the greatest of all risks that of giving ourselves away, is the only way of true art. Our literature is the literature of little things, not by reason of its subject, but because of the want of relation between the subject and the whole: between what we see and what there is to be seen. It is the proportions that matter. And if we deny ourselves the canvas of infinity, certain it is that small things will appear as great, futile things will appear as wise, and all be disorganized, because we have denied ourselves that element which alone could give true proportion.

The idea that poetry should be sublime has probably fallen into disrepute because something far from it was so often mistaken for the sublime. Sublimity has nothing to do with the grandiloquent, the pretentious, the rhetorical or the vague. Sublimity is nothing more than the extension of common view into the realms of wonder and of worship. Probably science had to do its work of showing us that the infinite lays beyond the very small, as well as beyond the very great, before we could get rid of merely rhetorical and obese ideas about sublimity. But nothing changes its nature by being wrongly named, and as in science inadequate ideas of matter give place, so current ideas in literature of the nature and worth of sublimity will be superseded.

Sublimity is the hall-mark of a great poet. It is the true distinction between the poet and the poetaster. The relation of the soul of man to infinity is obviously of greater ultimate concern to man than his relation to anything on earth. It is the ever-present sense of this relation that gives the poet his universal view. Indeed, but for the sense of infinity, knowledge would supersede poetry.

An infinite world being the soul's native region, matter therefore appearing to the soul as devoid of intrinsic worth, but only valuable as a means of expressing relative values, and William Blake desiring to write of the soul to the exclusion of all other themes, what option had he but to use symbols? They were inevitable. And as I hope I have already shown, they are an enrichment of poetry as poetry so long as they are symbols whose imagery is immediately recognizable. But what is to be said when they are not: when so far from being immediately recognizable they are completely unrecognizable and to the uninitiated, absolutely devoid of meaning? What is to be said in justification of them?

First, it must be insisted that Blake's use of such symbols was not arbitrary. Like Topsy, they "growed" and like Topsy they had a purpose in so doing. Blake was never intentionally mysterious. That sentence is worth repeating, because the contrary is so widely believed. Blake was never intentionally mysterious because he wrote to reveal and not to conceal, because, in fact, he was not a charlatan with a gullible public at his door clamouring to be mystified, but a poet without a single competent reader: a poet expressing, as explicitly as he could find words, what he believed to be truth. He wrote not, as the children say, "to appear big," but simply because he was big, and to complain that Blake was intentionally mysterious is to tell a giant that he appears to think himself big. Blake wrote of the deepest mysteries, but he wrote of them with all the clarity he could command, and his reply to the reverend gentleman who told him he needed somebody to elucidate his ideas, has a ring of indignation about it that ought to put to silence any suggestion that Blake belonged to the artful race of mystifies. "That which is grand," he replies, "is necessarily obscure to weak men. That which can be made explicit to the idiot is not worth my care. The wisest of the ancients considered what is not too explicit as fittest for instruction, because it rouses the faculties to act. I name Moses, Solomon, Æsop, Homer and Plato." On which the reverend gentleman's comment was, "Blake dim'd with superstition," a remark that has found many echoes in the halls of condescension.

But to be intentionally mysterious and to be "not too explicit" are not the same, the difference being between what is intentionally concealed and what is of free access to those who will help themselves.

If, however, Blake's symbols were not arbitrary, how did he come to use them?

We have glanced at the way they began. The further explanation is really simple and shows that, so far from being due to a love of mystery, they were due to the opposite cause: a meticulous care for precision.

When Blake took for his province the human soul he found it a world wholly unmapped and uncharted. Thereupon, with an exactitude which is baffling in its thoroughness, he set about making maps and charts of this undiscovered country. Being a poet and not merely a psychologist, he possessed to a peculiar degree that personalizing or anthropomorphic power which, for divine reasons, has always been the property of a poet. Moreover, Blake's faith in a spiritual as distinct from a natural world, was such that he believed all things were personalizations. He did not merely take attributes of the soul and give them names: for him these attributes, and indeed all things, had spiritual identity; and the power of seeing in distinct and minute details the spirit which informed the material substances he called "vision."

Illustration to Milton's "'L'Allegro"

In this design is introduced

Mountains on whose barren, breast
The labouring Clouds do often rest.

Mountains, Clouds, Rivers, Trees appear Humanized on the Sunshine Holiday. The Church Steeple with its merry bells. The Clouds arise from the bosoms of Mountains, While Two Angels sound their Trumpets in the Heavens to announce the Sunshine Holiday."—Blake's note.

Thus the creatures of his imagination were to him the realities of which any physical manifestation was only the shadow: the animating principle of an object was the spiritual source of its being. More and more he endeavoured to envisage the animating principle and not to be put off with material semblance, and he did not rest content until he saw the animating principles with such clearness of vision that each attained identity. When he found the identity he gave it a name.

That, I believe, is the true history of the growth of all Blake's symbols. They grew as his perceptive insight grew. He was a seer, or merely the most subjective of all poets, as you will; but that vexed question, begotten of our want of corresponding insight, as to whether his symbols made or marred his poetry, can only be answered satisfactorily when the whole of his vision has been seen.

4

A Reasonable Man

Q. Why is Blake like Underground?[1]
A. Because he is most enjoyable when he comes to the surface.

Which, if not quite true, is perhaps as true as the answers to most facetious riddles. Still, the analogy holds in many details. Blake became a subterranean poet because he could not get along quickly enough on the surface. There was congestion of the traffic with traditional ideas and many bad and useless effigies stood in the way. He did not mind going out of sight so long as he could construct his own routes, his object always being to arrive. Many have denied that Blake goes anywhere, except round the Inner Circle, but these have always been old ladies up from the country who have not dared to trust themselves to the lifts of Blake's symbolism, or, making a descent, have fallen asleep on the journey. But Blake had a terminus and many stations on the way, and just as the Underground offers to town-dwellers new opportunities for excursions in the country, so Blake carries his readers beyond the boundaries of the mundane shell more surely and quickly than any other English poet. We may prefer town: that is, we may prefer the order and discipline of the visible to the apparent disorder of the invisible, in which case Blake is maddening, for there is always a chance that we may get stuck in the tunnel, and then Blake is no joke to anyone. But while it remains true that he is most enjoyable when he emerges into the daylight of recognizable country, he remains about as valuable as the Underground stations would be without the railway if we are content to walk round him picking out the non-symbolic

1. American: subway.

plums. Every inch of his route is the result of hard boring through the dark clay and rock beneath our feet, and although the old ladies doubt it, the whole labyrinth is lit by the light of a superb intelligence.

Blake packed his wisdom into small parcels (this is true even of *Jerusalem*). He put the results of a tremendous lot of thinking on to some of his smallest pages, and as they are apt to be overlooked, Blake's power of pure intellect is also apt to be lost sight of. More especially is this the case since Blake himself relegated pure reason to an inferior place in the mind. He thought reason inferior to imagination, and if we lack higher gifts than reasoning ability we shall be inclined to think he could have had little of it who assigned to it a secondary place.

Blake's extreme concentration was largely due to the age in which he lived. His metal would probably never have contracted so suddenly had it not been exposed to extreme cold; but his mind was furnace hot and the air without icily unsympathetic. It is the speaker who cannot get a hearing who resorts to aphorisms: force that cannot find a vent expresses itself in explosion, and Blake was always exploding because his resistance to the lethargy that surrounded him was volcanic.

Then again, his native power of thinking for himself was never dulled. He was self-educated, and while he suffered many of the disabilities from which help at the right moment might have saved him, he escaped the even greater disabilities which help at the wrong moment confers. One of the most frequent disabilities of "the trained and disciplined mind" is a total loss of the power of thinking for itself. The mind that cannot grind its own corn, if well fed by a liberal education, becomes a barn of rotten wheat, and too many of these storehouses pass for intelligences. Blake could get nourishment out of bran. He ground it small, as his notes to Swedenborg show, and nothing that he read left him without bearing signs of having been through a powerful mill where it was forced to yield its last vitamin.

Finally, in any discussion about Blake's attitude to reason, we must never forget that much of what he said was in powerful reaction to the thought of his time. No one now thinks of reason or nature as a goddess, but Blake was writing when the Terror had made a temple for Reason and Rousseau was writing his

Confessions. Other times other names. Different powers of the mind in turn arrogate to themselves omniscience; different elements of what Blake called the Fourfold Man are always arising to claim the supremacy of divine right, and it may be that in our day we elevate instinct to the place which reason occupied at the end of the 18th century.

The processes in the development of Blake's mind are singularly interesting and easy to watch. He began with poetry—poetry that was derived, but not derived from the sluggish streams of his day. With fine instinct he went back to the freshest sources in English poesy and wrote in imitation of Shakespeare, Milton, Spenser and the old Balladists. This was the child learning to use speech by imitation of its parents—a very necessary process and one that deserves kinder treatment than it is won't to receive at the hands of grand-fatherly criticism. Criticism is so old: it mumbles away in the corner, intolerant of the interruptions of childish prattle or childish boastfulness. But since poets are not so much born as grown, those who desire the flower do well to encourage the imitative efforts essential to every kind of young life.

How finely young Blake did what had been done before him has barely been recognized. The lines "To Spring," "To the Evening Star," and "To the Muses" are not only beautiful, but they are also perfect after their kind and make the apology with which the *poetical Sketches* is prefaced cynically mirthful reading. "Conscious of the irregularities and defects to be found on almost every page" elderly patronage usually is, but it seems strange now that this book could have been seen by any but Blake without being acclaimed.

How did its reception strike him? Did he mind this damning with faint praise? Was he glad the book went without recognition? It is recorded that he took no pains to sell it himself; but that of itself is rather poor evidence that he was not disappointed with its reception. Where is the young poet who is anxious to hawk his work like a gipsy? If Blake did not suffer from his cold reception he was the first of his kind to show such equanimity, and insensitiveness to neglect is certainly not one of the virtues—if virtue it be— that Blake's later behaviour would lead us to suppose he possessed in his teens.

A far finer virtue he did possess and in glorious measure. That was the ability to keep his eye on the mark in front of him and not to weep, to the dimming of that eye, over spilt milk. In the years that immediately followed, Blake found himself, and thus we come to the second stage of his mental growth.

He became intellectually clear-sighted; that is to say, he learnt to distinguish his own thoughts from those transferred to him by reading, or by contact with other minds such as Paine's or Godwin's, or any of the other members of the fraternity that patronized the publisher Johnson. He achieved what he would have called Single Vision, which may be interpreted as pure mental) sensation: the power of true mental reaction to whatever comes before the mind. The proper medium for this reflex is prose, more especially in the form of criticism, since the mental eye so employed is not dynamic but selective.

At this stage, Blake wrote those important aphorisms, entitled *There is No Natural Religion* and *All Religions are One*. He also wrote *An Island in the Moon* (at the end of which we see him entering upon a further stage) and probably a good number of the "Proverbs of Hell" afterwards incorporated in *The Marriage of Heaven and Hell.*

The *Tractates*, as they have been called, are so slight in bulk that their importance has been rather overlooked. Here Blake compressed his thought to the point of ellipsis, partly, of course, because he wanted to use small plates to test his invention in printing, but also because thought that has lacked expression for a number of years, as Blake's had, and at the same time has been vigorous, tends to become aphoristic. But these tiny plates are very important, for with them Blake laid the foundations of all that he afterwards built, and from the conclusions there arrived at he never departed. It is interesting to note in passing that he headed the third series "The voice of one crying in the Wilderness." He had been in the wilderness since he wrote the *Poetical Sketches* and he realized his solitude.

The lyrics at the end of *An Island in the Moon* that were afterwards included in the *Songs of Innocence* indicate the next change. Blake has come back to poetry again, but this time it is no longer imitative poetry, it is supremely his own. Here he enters upon "Two-fold Vision," or intellectual understanding as distinguished from mere sight. The image here is "two-fold always" and being the image of childhood does not awake that emotional concord and discord which is characteristic of the stage that follows. This is the poetry of Eden and in point of intellectual happiness marks a stage not to be transcended. But it is the most transient of all and is quickly superseded by understanding that takes emotional cognizance and is Love, in the comprehensive sense in which Love includes both Sight and Intellectual Understanding. This is "three-fold vision," the stage of Blake's growth when he wrote the *Songs of Experience,* and all the smaller prophetic books. "Soft Beulah's Night," he calls it; but while it is sustained by a sympathy not intelligible to either of the former stages, it represents intellectually the travail of the soul in its incarnation, and not only the delights but "the torments of love and jealousy."

The last stage in the growth of Blake's mind is difficult to describe, though easy to indicate. It was achieved while he was at Felpham, and his amazing record of the illumination is given in one of the poems he sent to Captain Butts. In "fourfold vision" the war of the senses has ceased. Intellectual and emotional understanding have given place to something even higher, and the Sage, or Seer, or Spiritual Visionary is born. Imagination, which is the means, has achieved Vision, which is the end, as Imagination is courtship, and Vision marriage. The image and object are one: identity is universally perceived: the spiritual reality is no longer an appearance that emerges from the veil at moments of happy insight: it presents itself everywhere in the form of "naked beauty displayed." "Four-fold vision" sees every living thing as it is in its eternal reality. To Blake, science represented the bones of the human body, reason the bones clothed in flesh, imagination the living form, and vision the human form divine.

Poets are ordinary men of heightened susceptibility. It is a vulgar error to think of them as a race apart and of their experiences as peculiar. Their experiences are only peculiar in their intensity; essentially these experiences are common to all. The path of understanding which Blake took is the common highway, and the difference between his experience and ours is only a difference of intensity due to the fact that he trod the road with spiritual eyes wide open and human senses keen.

Single Vision is the state we suffer when the soul sleeps and appearances form themselves on the mind's eye like images on a photographic plate.

Two-fold Vision is our state when the intellect is active and our interest in appearances is scientific. Here knowledge reigns and we have intellectual understanding.

Three-fold Vision is ours when the heart's knowledge is added to the minds. Here imagination is born. We suffer and enjoy and feelingly express our understanding.

Four-fold Vision is spiritual insight: the power to perceive divine reality. It comes when the imagination has completed its work in us. It is the soul's triumph when the action of the senses is synthetic.

But what do we mean by reality? Reality is another of those terms that make us sigh for a fresh vocabulary, because the word conveys so many different meanings.

Fortunately there is no doubt about what reality meant to Blake. It was for him the universal soul of man. That was for him the only reality: all else was a product, or "emanation" of that soul. He conceived of reality as eternal form, contrasted with unreality which was temporal appearance.

This is an inversion of common thought. We speak of the "reality" of a thing when we mean its material substance. That was exactly what Blake meant by its unreality or shadow. The corporeal form, the vegetative nature, were for him the partial or sensory impressions made by appearance on eyes that were glasses of reflection instead of being dynamic organs of sight. Whatever appeared on those glasses of reflection was delusion or unreality. True perception had sight of the eternal form.

Blake, we have said, laid the foundations of his philosophy in those three short *Tractates* which were his first essays in etched printing. It is significant that in the first series the word "perceive," or its variants, appears in every one of the six corollaries. Clearly it is no objective truth he is questing here. He desires not merely to see, but to apprehend with the mind.

If the universal soul of man was to be the theme of all his poetry and the true subject of all his drawings, the first thing to be discovered was whether such a soul existed. And this he set about to demonstrate to the rational mind in the workmanlike manner of Euclid.

There is nothing equivocal about his title. "There is no Natural Religion" states the case without any fine shades of dialectical meaning. But if there was no natural religion, there were plenty of natural religionists in Blake's day. The time was the time of Paine, Rousseau and Voltaire. Others like-minded in this country formed a circle of free-thinkers which once included Blake—if any circle can be said to have ever included him. Anyway, he soon became an apostate, and as the apostate is always the fiercest foe, lake's onslaught was not wanting in vigour.

In the First Series he begins by accepting common ground with the Natural Religionists and stating what would be acceptable to them, namely, that "Man has no notion of moral fitness but from Education. Naturally he is only a natural organ subject to Sense." Upon this postulate he argues the case in the negative by making six corollaries. He then draws a conclusion, and his conclusion is that "If it were not for the Poetic or Prophetic character, the Philosophic and Experimental would soon be at the ratio of all things and stand still, unable to do other than repeat the same dull round over again." His object here is to prove that if man is nothing but a natural organ subject to sense—if indeed the finite is the limit of his perceptions—then the relativity of finite objects is the whole problem of existence.

To prove the contrary he lays down six propositions which State his case in the affirmative, and the first of these propositions is, that "Man's perceptions are not bounded by organs of perception: he perceives more than sense (though ever so acute) can discover."

That was perhaps the most important conclusion Blake ever reached. With that sentence he lays the corner-stone of his philosophy, makes his vindication of the spiritual world, and asserts the supremacy of the imagination over every other faculty in man. Here he definitely places the imagination outside the reach of the five senses as a power which, though it works through them, is not subject to their bonds. "The true method of knowledge," he says in the next axiom, "is experiment." By contrast, the power which perceives beyond knowledge, is imagination. If man is able to perceive more than sense can demonstrate, he must be able to do this by a power greater than sense perception: this power Blake calls imagination.

> How do you know but ev'ry Bird that cuts the airy way?
> Is an immense world of delight, clos'd by your senses five?

When Blake wrote that there was probably not a man beside himself but would have smiled over such an amiable fancy, putting it in the category of such bright suppositions as, if pigs had wings. But now, while our so-called religious leaders would probably deny the question any relevance to the foundations of faith, every respectable scientist is able to explain just how the bird contains within its material body molecules each of which is a solar system, and not only "an immense world of delight," but a Milky Way of worlds, whose delight or despair must still be left to the imagination.

Thus wisdom is justified of her children.

But what is imagination? Another of those words that are all things to all men. Imagination has been made a terrible maid-of-all-work. It does duty for hallucination, phantasy, fancy, error, hypothesis, suspicion, thought, and even brain: indeed, so wide is its application and so varied its meanings both high and low, you may judge a man's whole character by his use of that one word. To Blake it came to stand for all that is most beautiful and holy in this or in any other world. Hence the importance of noting how carefully he defended his reverence for this power, here at the outset of his career as an imaginative artist. Himself so soon to leave the wearisome and futile pursuit of truth by the way of logic, it is worthwhile pausing to see just what powers of reason he could put forth in defence of his faith.

Before leaving this first proposition we may observe that the motto to *Visions of the Daughters of Albion* is the same statement put more succinctly. This motto has been badly misunderstood. It has been interpreted as Blake's confession that he did not always understand what his visions signified! Which, as Euclid says, is absurd. "The eye sees more than the heart knows" is only an imaginative way of saying man "perceives more than sense can discover." The eye, the light of the mind, is the symbol of spiritual perception or imagination: the heart, the primary organ of the body, is the symbol of sense. Imagination comprehends more than Love. Vision transcends Experience.

The remaining propositions are fairly self-evident with the exception of number five:

"If the many become the same as the few when possess'd, More! More! is the cry of a mistaken soul; less than all cannot satisfy Man."

There is definite ellipsis here. What Blake is showing is that if this world were bounded by the finite, Man's inherent desire for increase would be a mistake; but his desires being infinite, nothing less than the Infinite can satisfy him. If we transpose the tense and expand a little, his meaning becomes clear. 'If much, when possessed, became the same as little, when possessed, More! More! would be the cry of a mistaken soul. It is not, because less than all cannot satisfy man.' The conclusion is that "The desire of Man being Infinite, the possession is Infinite and himself Infinite."

What does this imply? It implies that man is not merely "a natural organ subject to sense," but a living soul which has God for its possession and is itself of the divine nature. Whence we pass on to the "Application: He who sees the Infinite in all things, sees God. He who sees the Ratio only, sees himself only. Therefore God becomes as we are, that we may be as he is."

All attempts to define God (and Blake would have added, or Man) must fail. They must fail because God is not a fact but an imaginative reality, and an imaginative reality is the subject of perception but never of proof; Blake never drew a line where God ended and Man began. The nearest he approaches to definition of deity is perhaps in the early lines of *Vala, or The Tour Zoos* where he speaks of "the Universal Brotherhood of Eden, The Universal Man, To Whom be Glory Evermore," or in the second stanza of "The Divine Image":

For Mercy, Pity, Peace and Love
Is God our father dear,
And Mercy, Pity, Peace and Love
Is Man, his child and care.

The nearest we will approach to objective statement of Blake's idea is this: God is Infinite Man: Man confined to the senses is Finite God. Man becomes as God when he apprehends as God apprehends. He confines himself to the limitations of mortality when he lives by reason and not by imagination, thus neglecting to use his God-given means to apprehension of the Infinite.

Thus by applying the processes of logic to matters too high for prose we approach the region of metaphysics. Only once more—in *All Religions are One*—did Blake attempt to define by statement "the very image of life," which can only be "expressed in its eternal truth" by poetry. But in the process, as in the examples we have studied, he demonstrated for the benefit of those to whom it is of concern that he possessed reasoning faculty in a very high degree.

It has perhaps been worthwhile labouring this point because Blake is sometimes ignorantly regarded as a person of hazy "mystical" ideas who had no use for reason and was therefore proudly unreasonable. The contrary is the truth. Because he was able to think with great clarity he saw the limits of logic and put reason in the hierarchy of intelligence where every good thinker has put it, under the guidance of poetry. Though he attacked reason's usurpation of the seat of spiritual intelligence, he would as soon have cast instinct and emotion out of the places of equality he assigned to them in the composition of the true man, as leave out this part of intelligence. Only those capable of using reason in a high degree will be able fully to appreciate his consistent reasonableness; for Blake was busy with things beyond reason and he did not trail his coat.

5

The Circle of Happiness

Blake was one of the happiest of mortals. He began singing when he was twelve and he literally died singing.

When he was about fifty, he said of himself:

> The Angel that presided o'er my birth
> Said, "Little creature form'd of Joy and Mirth,
> Go love without the help of anything on earth."

He believed that he came from "Eden, the land of delight" and that "conversations concerning Mental Delights" was one of the occupations of the inhabitants of Eternity. His autobiography is that of a happy man. Here it is, as he wrote it the year before he died:

> "William Blake—one who is very much delighted with being in good company. Born on 28th November, 1757, in London, and has died several times since."

"If asked," wrote Samuel Palmer, "whether I ever knew among the intellectual a happy man, Blake would be the only one who would immediately occur to me."

Blake enjoyed to the full the happiness of the child, which is the joy of self-assertion, the joy which the seed has when it germinates and thrusts shoots above the mould; but he also knew, what is rare, the happiness of age, which is the joy of humility. It took several deaths to teach a man of Blake's individual pride that joy; but he had the energy to learn it. For three-quarters of his life he continued to put forth his highest efforts in the belief that someone would recognize and appreciate them. His hope of much material benefits soon vanished, but he continued to believe that in the end someone would have a just appreciation of what he could not help knowing was of great value. Yet as the years passed he became known, not as a sublime artist and the greatest poet of his age, but as a cantankerous oddity. Publishers and public alike treated him with contempt. Friends with whom he had set out in high hope began to look askance and offer patronizing advice, or to forget him altogether. Undaunted he worked on with greater zeal than ever. It was of no avail. His name was now associated with failure. He became the object of public and private charity. To the very end no one understood, no one even appreciated the significance of his *Songs of Innocence,* and he died a child of the artistic poor-law, that is, one who receives for his work payment which is given more out of humane than out of artistic consideration. Oddly enough, society is still constituted so as to make this manner of living appear the extremity of humiliation.

The consolations of artistic failure—a happy family, an assured income, opportunities for travel, even a back garden—Blake had none of these. His art was his life and the world would have none of it. He was even forced to sell the only possessions he ever treasured—a bundle of old prints. This is the man who had written:

> The Sun does arise
> And make happy the skies.
> The merry bells ring
> To welcome the Spring.
> The skylark and thrush,
> The birds of the bush,
> Sing louder around
> To the bells' cheerful sound,
> While our sports shall be seen
> On the Echoing Green.

But he died happier than that. He died experiencing the divine happiness revealed in those last five plates of *Jerusalem,* than which a more sublime and perfect happiness has never found literary expression.

Blake's original happiness was the happiness of every lyrical poet and indeed the happiness common in measure to all that is young. The *Songs of Innocence* are the inestimable treasure they are because they express what is so rare in this world—unalloyed, self-dependent happiness. In the *Songs of Innocence*

Blake made a discovery. He discovered childhood. He was the first to announce it. Hitherto, childhood had been regarded merely as a state of immature growth. He showed it to be a condition of happiness, unity and self-enjoyment; a sunrise which enables us to see the Glory of God and the original state of the soul.[1]

Without the sense of happiness, lyrical poetry cannot be written. That is not to say that lyrical poetry is the poetry of happiness; on the contrary, we know what the subject of our sweetest songs is: but without the sense of happiness, or consciousness of an ideal state, saddest thought, which only gains its sweetness by contrast, would have no background and be indistinguishable from abysmal misery. It does not matter whether the poet expresses happiness, like Blake, or unhappiness, like Shelley: without the sense of happiness neither would be vocal; for lyrical poetry is man's supreme attestation to the worth of life, and the idea that life is of priceless value is latent in every genuine lyric. Lyrical poets are those who retain that sense of happiness longest. They retain the power of spontaneous enjoyment longer than their fellows because the original force they bring into life is greater.

The passage of our life between birth and adolescence is like the passage of a vessel down a river. We go with the stream no matter what winds may blow or how the rain falls. From day to day the scene changes: there is no sameness, for the very physical inches we attain alter the outlook. The more we keep to mid-stream the faster we go, and all the time there lies before us the alluring prospect of the sea.

Then suddenly we are at the river mouth. The current that bore us ceases, and in its stead are waves and adverse tides. The course we followed without choice is at an end, and here are wide illimitable waters where if we are to find direction at all it must be from charts that lie within the vessel itself. What was a friendly element seems suddenly to have become an enemy threatening us with disaster? Now we may shout for aid and

1. Unorganiz'd Innocence An Impossibility.
Innocence dwells with Wisdom, but never with Ignorance.
A Note on one of the pages of "The Four Zoas"

guidance as we will, the gentle riverbanks are gone and with them the voices that used to reply.

Happy are they who sail mid-stream—those in whom the tide of life runs so strongly they are carried over the shoals of self-consciousness without loss of original force. Such are lyrical poets. They retain their sense of the divine origin of life, despite the pressure of environment upon them. The soul that rises with them continues to shine long after it has faded for most of their fellows.

But though they retain the sense of happiness long after self-consciousness has brought its equivocations into the souls of most men—though for a moment they retard the coming of Time and reveal Eternity by enabling us to see the world with eyes undimmed by doubt, the vision of innocence has never been retained by any poet who lived a normal term of years.

Why is this? Why shouldn't a poet sustain lyrical impulse till he died of old age?

Simply because there is more than one of us in this world. The happiness of a child is by nature selfish and instinctive. The child lives for itself: self-increase is normally its whole object, and woe betide us if we thwart the child in this pursuit and mutilate the infant mind with grown ideas of happiness and altruism. But at maturity we have the opportunity of experiencing happiness of a greater capacity than can be known by a child: happiness that is not selfish and instinctive, but inclusive and imaginative. Beyond the realm of childhood, unalloyed self-dependent happiness is not to be found, because, while the child lives as a unit only appreciating society as a means of gratifying its wants, at adolescence we come into the possession of powers which, for their natural enjoyment, depend upon the delights and desires of others. That which in any measure depends for its fulfillment upon others can no longer be described as "self-dependent."

Thus our original happiness is impossible, because two people cannot possess the same thing at the same time without sharing it. The happiness of childhood differs from the happiness of maturity in that childish happiness is the happiness of possession, while the happiness of maturity is the joy of sharing. That we should try to gain childish happiness when we come to maturity is one of the misfortunes of delayed growth and a very pregnant cause of the world's woes. But at adolescence we bump into the world as a social organism: the "not-ourselves" has to be recognized, and never yet has this stage of life been encountered without pain and loss of original happiness.

From this pain and loss Blake, though he has appeared in the world's eye for a hundred years as the supreme poet of youthful happiness, was not immune. On the contrary, having an immense capacity for childish happiness, he sustained the loss of it with all the suffering that the law of reaction makes inevitable. His sense of dismay at having passed for ever out of his Eden was so acute that it took form and presented itself to him as a state incident to every human life. That state he named Experience.

Experience is a state of disillusionment. The soul that ran to embrace the world with open arms is rebuffed: it discovers in Matthew Arnold's words that

> . . . the world, which seems
> To lie before us like a land of dreams,
> So various, so beautiful, so new,
> Hath really neither joy, nor love, nor light.
> Nor certitude, nor peace, nor help for pain.

Corruption lies at the roots of life. Cruelty is universal. The innocent lamb is the prey of the lion. Hunger, pain and deceit dog the steps of every living thing. Jealousy shadows love. Faith appears as man's pathetic refusal to face facts: hope, the illusion he pursues flying in terror from fear.

Blake's image of this state was the grave. Nothing but death was catastrophic enough to symbolize this negation of all that made life good. But, as with many of Blake's symbols, the grave was not merely a symbol, it was an image. Seen with the eyes of the soul, this total loss of joy, the soul's life, *is* death, the only form of death the soul can know.

Physiologically this state occurs when self-sufficiency is no longer possible to the body. At adolescence, the subconscious mind of youth realizes that the independence now required of it, as never before, has no physiological basis. The body has acquired powers that have no meaning except in relation to another, and the sense of desire, without an object for that desire, drives the force back upon itself and creates the dualism within which we call self-consciousness.

In Blake's time there were philosophers who argued that this state of experience was to be avoided by rational education. They wanted to see the course of youth flow on through adolescence with undiminished power, and this they believed would happen if the facts of life, and especially of sex, were not veiled in mystery. They believed that the pains of self-consciousness were due to ignorance, which was preventable. They were the Deists or Natural Religionists.

Blake regarded their opinions as "of fatal and accursed consequence to man." He described their state of mind as "Rahab" and called it an eternal state, meaning thereby that theirs was a form of error which under other names would always exist to seduce man from the truth. He saw that what they really desired was to perpetuate the state of Innocence, and while none could love Innocence better than Blake, he understood that unless man passed out of Innocence through Experience to Imagination, society could be nothing but the congregation of disparate units, each warring in defence of its own life. Seeing more clearly than they, he perceived that however the difficulties of self-consciousness were modified by education, adolescence would still denote the entrance of another principle of being into the individual—a principal that implied change of direction and necessitated a new orientation towards the world for as simple a reason as the fact that when Eve joined Adam in the Garden of Eden, nothing was ever the same again. Understanding childhood, Blake saw that if the grown individual could persist beyond childhood without self-consciousness, all his actions would be rapacious; or to express the matter in his own phraseology, that the self, instead of becoming emanative, would be shut up-in selfhood unable to know friendship or brotherhood, without which, he roundly declared, "Man is not."

To be shut up in selfhood was Blake's idea of hell. As early as 1788 we find him noting in his copy of Lavater's *Aphorisms on Man* that "hell is the being shut up in the possession of corporeal desires." Crucifixion, death and the descent into hell he understood as imaginative images of the progress of every soul in this world. The question for him was not whether men went to hell, but how they got out of it, and it was to show this that he wrote *Vala, or The Four Zoos* where the theme is:

> His fall into Division and his Resurrection to Unity:
> His fall into the Generation of decay and death, and his
> Regeneration by the Resurrection from the dead.

and *Jerusalem* which tells

> Of the Sleep of Ulro! and of the passage through
> Eternal Death! and of the awaking to Eternal Life.

Blake's answer was that the principle by which man perceives what is beyond the realm of sense, the principle by which he perceives the Infinite in all things, is "the power of God unto salvation."

> When weary Man enters his Cave
> He meets his Saviour in the Grave.

The moment when self-sufficiency fails, when God is no longer mediated by the love and care of human parents and the soul stands between two eternities uncertain to which it belongs, is the moment when Imagination waits to link the soul's life with all that is beyond itself. Henceforward there can be only two ways: the way of death which is the predatory exertion of the self after Innocence has been passed, or the way of life which is the way of Imagination.

As an artist Blake's idea of Imagination was of the power by which he was enabled to perceive true identities. Imagination gave living form as distinct from mere resemblance. Similarly the purpose of Imagination in man was to give to every man true knowledge of his own identity. The soul which came from God as essence passed through a series of states in this life in order that it might achieve individual identity. But it was cardinal in Blake's mind that without Imagination the individual remained in the grave of self. Hence the sharpness of his division from the Deists who, like the Sadducees of old, denied the resurrection.

The "analysis" and "sublimation" of our own day are variations on the same theme. One is tempted to believe that Blake knew all about psycho-analysis when he wrote:

> Why wilt thou examine every little fibre of my soul
> Spreading them out before the sun like stalks of flax
> to dry?

The infant joy is beautiful, but its anatomy
Horrible, Ghast and Deadly: nought shalt thou find in it
But Death, Despair and everlasting brooding Melancholy.
Thou wilt go mad with horror if thou dost examine thus
Every moment of my secret hours.

For him Experience was the test of the soul's honesty. Once it was reached the soul went forward to Imagination or backward to Memory. If the soul could persuade itself that it might by any means return to Innocence, the honesty of that soul was destroyed, and before it lay the long and dismal journey of self-contradiction in the pursuit of chimeras (such chimeras, one may opine, as "complete analysis") before it could return to the place where it parted from its integrity.[1]

Blake saw the inevitable association of Deism —of the Christianity of Ten Commandments and of what we may now call Behaviourism—with that which he held in greatest abhorrence, Moral Law. Moral Law was the antithesis of Imagination, for it was the imposition from without of general form upon that which had its own inherent individual form. If everything that lived was holy, how could holiness be thrust upon it as a garment? The God of Christendom he called: "An Abstract objecting power that negatives everything," and the business which has for its end the perfect adaptation of the individual to his environment would have alike met with his derision. The "normal man" of modern psychology would have been Blake's name for a human nonentity.

He believed that all such religion was false, because it encouraged the selfhood, or loveless ego, to live in false humility aping Innocence. All such religion he called the Religion of Hypocrisy. It was the pretence to peace between the soul of man and nature red in tooth and claw, when there was no peace. It was the pretence to harmony between the facts of experience and the truth of the soul, when there was no such harmony. It

1. The couplet "An Answer to the Parson" suggests that Blake was asked by a clergyman of his day why he did not join the Fold. The question as he puts it: "Why of the sheep do you not learn peace?" might be interpreted: "Why don't you return to the state of Innocence?" But Blake's symbol of Innocence was the lamb whose habits are pretty but not to be copied, while those of the sheep are proverbially imitation and stupidity.

was the denial of Imagination, which perceived more than sense (tho' ever so acute) could discover, by that rationalizing process which desired to embrace the universe in the logic of one mind.

He would have none of it. Blake went to the bottom of the grave of experience, and when he rose again, he did not confound his spiritual body with the linen clothes he had left behind. "To rise from generation free," he tells us in the poem addressed to the mother of his mortality, "what-e'er is born of mortal birth must be consumed with the Earth." As Jesus died to mortal life that he might rise to spiritual life (Blake quotes: "It is raised a spiritual body" on his design to this poem) so the soul in the moment of its awakening to imaginative life dies to the life of nature, leaving Innocence behind it as the grave-clothes.

Thenceforward the secret of Blake's happiness was vision. He believed that men became what they beheld: hence his one desire was to see truly in order that he himself might be an image of the truth. What he saw filled him with worship, and his life became one sustained effort to give appropriate form to that which so delighted his spiritual eye. He was happy in the exercise of his imagination, and for man in maturity he knew of no other enjoyable way of living.

Blake did not, as has been said, "announce the religion of art." He regarded art as the inevitable product of vision, but vision was both means and end. The distinction is important. Vision is the immaterial apprehension of truth. Art is the material record of that apprehension. Nothing material could have ever formed the foundation of Blake's religion. He justified the works of Imagination in an age when they were regarded as the foundlings of idle fancy; but he never toppled over into the pitiable error which distracted the aesthetes of the 19th century, of believing that art was anything but a human record of the perception of truth. To confound the thing made with the imaginative reality and give to that made, the devotion and worship due to that which makes, is idolatry that rots the soul. Blake taught no such heresy. Works of art he strove to make unceasingly because love prompts action, but never did he remotely confound the image he was able to trace and the object of his love and worship.

But every man, just in so far as he is not a poet (using that word in its widest and truest sense) is a descendant of Pilate, for truth of some kind the mind must have, and if it is not the truth of poetry then it will be the truth according to law. Jesus acted directly but spoke indirectly by parables. When we do not apprehend the truth as poets apprehend, we feel we should prefer that Jesus had spoken directly and acted—as we even come to think he acted—parabolically. Why couldn't he have said what he meant and told men their duty in plain terms, instead of wrapping it all up in these parables of good Samaritans and grains of mustard seed? Then we could have tabled the seven deadly sins and fixed a code of behaviour that would have ensured to us the good things all men desire of this life and any other. And many, thinking thus, have translated the poetry of religion into their own legal prose. In so doing they have cursed the world with another substitute for truth.

Truth cannot be circumscribed. When Jesus described himself as the truth, we do not suppose that his physical body became the residuum of truth, but rather that in him truth found a focal point: he was the translucent prism of light, the means whereby light was made humanly appreciable. He was not a vessel which blotted out the sun by absorption. Pilate wanted the sun to come within his orbit. He did not see that his orbit shut out the sun.

His error lies persistently in wait for the reader of Blake, because of the unique degree to which Blake relied upon direct apprehension. Blake did not even try to understand the universe by the ordinary processes of reasonable deduction; yet, if the analogy may be pardoned, as the actions of Jesus were intelligible to the people who benefited by them while his words were a perpetual offence, so below the realm of Blake the visionary lies the plane of Blake the profoundly reasonable man; and seizing with our reasoning faculties upon his apparent reasonableness we are often tempted to believe the rest of his work is merely a puzzle to which he failed to supply the clue. When a man could express himself as intelligibly as Blake in the "Proverbs of Hell," what but madness and delusion could have made him the elusive creature of symbolism?

There speaks sound common sense—and Pilate. Poetry is not the vehicle of sound common sense, but is a means of creating images, which like the prism, ray out innumerable aspects of

6

Two Examples

When Pilate, proudly, cynically, or with humble curiosity, put before Jesus the famous question, "What is truth?" he did the human race the greatest service that it lay in his power to perform? He apotheosized the reasoning faculty. At a crucial moment he put the crucial question. For if Jesus had been able to give a purely reasonable and wholly adequate answer to that question, not only Christianity, but every religion in the world would have been rendered superfluous. If, by an effort of reason, man could in any wise encompass truth, then at that moment the perceptive or imaginative faculty of mankind would fall into abeyance; the riddle of the universe would be solved and, incidentally, man would lose his reason: it would die of starvation.

Of course, Pilate had for the moment forgotten himself. He was the representative of Roman law and, as the emissary of Law, facts and not the truth were his business. But Pilate's furtive soul crept out and made an infantile gesture, and by that gesture revealed forever the impassable chasm that divides facts from truth. The world has been profiting by his moment of forgetfulness ever since; and though the Law still asks its witnesses to deliver "the truth, the whole truth, and nothing but the truth," no one is fool enough to suppose the Law to mean what it says, for everyone knows that it merely requires the facts even when they belie the truth. At Pilate's historic moment the embodiment of truth stood before the embodiment of reason and the challenge to truth was merely that of making itself explicable. This Truth failed to do, with consequences that turned the world upside down. Never again has it been possible for a reasonable being to suppose that truth can be encompassed by facts, though Science has had moments of delusion.

truth. Blake did not choose from an alternative to write in verse: he wrote in verse because poetry was the only adequate means of conveying what he perceived. It was not optional to him whether he should set out his philosophy in reasonable terms, or whether he should leave us to deduce his philosophy when our apprehensions failed to pursue his in the quest of vision; and the fact that must be grasped is that apart from the poetry which contains his ideas, what he wrote is, and will forever remain, utterly unintelligible. It must remain unintelligible for this, the profoundest of all reasons, that poetry is an image of truth, and philosophy a rational statement of intellectual ideas. The greater contains the less, but not *vice versa.* Our perception of truth is not dependent upon fact, but upon intensity of imagination, and what Blake ultimately demands, and so far, has demanded in vain, is power of vision equal to his own. The poet appeals to his peers.

It is necessary to say this because a little knowledge of Blake usually leads us to believe the fallacy that one very fine day we shall discover, or some other person who has been equally enchanted by Blake, will discover, the key to Blake—a key that will open all the hidden doors and let us into the two-and-thirty palaces like children following a guide at Hampton Court. We come to think of Blake as a sort of glorious conundrum which one day will be wholly and finally solved. And I verily believe that publishers and critics are at this moment keenly on the look-out for the book which promises some such grand solution.

They will look in vain. There is no such key. Blake is bigger and better than that. He lived in a realm we only enter at the happiest moments of insight. He habitually used a tongue we only speak at rare moments of keenest understanding. He flew where we walk or are wheeled in perambulators. He fed on manna while we soon cry out for solid quails. He moved about at ease in worlds unrecognized and gazed upon the sun's face almost without a veil.

This is perceived by those who understand him a little. By others it is denied: the irrational Blake is for them a man lost in his own terminology; but, like Vala destroying her heart's desire, they "only see his feet like pillars of fire travelling through darkness and non-entity."

It is perhaps time to justify such professions of faith, and this can best be done by instancing discoveries that have opened magic casements, not indeed in the belief that perception is a quality whose enjoyment can be communicated, but simply in the hope of showing that Blake is worth all the understanding we can give him. I must apologize for so doing, because there is no duller occupation than watching an angler, though few recreations are more enjoyable than landing one's own fish. Moreover, in Blake's great rivers there is room for any number of rods, and, be it noted, there are no reaches reserved for scholarship. He who declares he has fished a spot empty shows himself to be using the wrong bait.

Title-Page of "The Book of Thel"

Let us take the title page of *The Book of Thel.* It is a happy example of Blake's power of concentration. On the left of the page, beneath a tall sapling, arched so deeply that it embraces the whole design, stands a young girl with a shepherd's crook in her left hand. Her features bear an expression of reproach, for she turns to watch two tiny figures that have just escaped from the opening flowers. The male figure leaps to embrace the female, who raises her arms in a gesture of surprise and alarm. Above them, the arch formed by the tree is full of birds and other figures expressive of innocent delight: the letters of the title themselves put forth leaves.

This picture epitomizes the exquisite narrative poem that follows. The girl is Thel. She is full grown; but anything that pertains to the shepherd's calling is for Blake a symbol of innocence; so Thel must be the representative of adolescent youth. This is confirmed by the sapling under which she stands. Blake invariably uses the tree as a symbol of generation, and whatever stands beneath a tree is under the shadow of mortal life. Thel's tree, though young, is sadly bent, and is thus an apt emblem of the disillusionment and melancholy that come to youth at first sight of experience. And the sight of experience is what Thel has as she stands watching the nuptials of the flowers.

Thel has been thought to be "a spirit not yet generated" and her experience, the descent into this world. But apart from our reading of the illustration, the opening lines of the poem quickly make it clear that Thel is already in this world. 'Tis from her "*mortal* day" she seeks to fade. "Our spring" is the time of childhood, and the watery bow, the cloud, the reflection in a glass, the shadow, and the dream, to all of which she likens herself, are all images of mortality. Those who heard "the voice of Him that walked in the garden in the Evening time," though still in Eden, were generated mortals. *The Book of Thel* stands between the *Songs of Innocence* and the *Songs of Experience*, and that is Thel's position; between the two states. Innocence stands on the threshold of Experience.

What is the meaning of Thel's motto?

> Does the Eagle know what is in the pit,
> Or wilt thou go ask the Mole?
> Can Wisdom be put in a silver rod?
> Or Love in a golden bowl?

The eagle has the eye that can gaze upon the sun: the mole is reputed to be blind and lives underground. A cross-reference to a passage in *Visions of the Daughters of Albion* gives us,

> Does not the Eagle scorn the earth and despise the
> treasures beneath?
> But the Mole knoweth what is there and the worm
> shall tell it thee.

So the contrast is evidently between what is above the earth and what is beneath it, and we know that everywhere in Blake what is above the earth has spiritual significance and what is within, or beneath it, symbolizes the instinctive or generative powers. The sun, which in "The Little Black Boy" of the *Songs of Innocence* is the place where

> God does live
> And gives his light and gives his heat away,

is Blake's symbol of spiritual light; and is contrasted with the fires "that belch incessant from the summits of the earth." Hence we may suggest, with the partiality which is inherent in all prose renderings of poetry, the content of the first two lines to be something like this:

> Does spiritual life know of generation?
> Seek that in the blind instinctive life of the earth.

There now remain the symbols of the silver rod and the golden bowl. Silver is throughout Blake associated with the light of the moon, and gold with the light of the sun. Urizen, Prince of Light, has a golden crown. Luvah, Prince of Love, has a silver bow. Hence, gold is a metal of the mind, and silver a metal of the loins. From which we may infer this meaning:

> Can Wisdom (man's highest good) be found in the organ
> of procreation,
> Or Love (woman's life) be contained in the womb?

This motto has not the universal meaning of the motto to *Visions of the Daughters of Albion:* "The Eye sees more than the Heart knows." It is Thel's motto, not Blake's. There were treasures in the earth Thel had yet to discover, treasures which Oothoon (who is really Thel at a later stage) found despite her sufferings; but while Thel's motto does not deny the purpose or value of Experience, it suggests with great power Blake's fundamental belief in the unity and integrity of the soul apart from mortal life.

With sure instinct Blake shows the burden of Thel's grief to be the sense of her own mortality. Self-consciousness is an eating of the Tree of Knowledge—knowledge of separate individuality and hence isolation from surrounding life and consequent realization of death. So, from the Lily, the Cloud, the Worm and the Clod of Clay, Thel learns to understand that this isolation is but an appearance: all life is spiritual and therefore eternal: the meanest thing that lives owes its maintenance to divine prevision. As soon as Thel understands this, her fear of mortality is quelled. But now the matron Clay offers to show her the secrets of generative life in those caverns of the earth where the fires of instinct rage. She invites Thel to enter imaginatively, and not actually, and thus to retain her freedom to return to Innocence unharmed.

Immediately there is a change in the whole tenor of the poem. The words no longer ripple and flow like the tide of light at sunrise; dark clouds and a biting wind have suddenly sprung up. The keeper of the gates of vision lifts the bar that divides the spiritual from the instinctive world. Thel enters in and looks upon the realm that Blake afterwards identifies as Hell. She wanders on until she comes to "her own grave-plot" and her vision there is of her own descent into the pit of generation. From this, that the Eagle knows not of, a voice arraigns the five senses telling of the deceits of love in the flesh. This is more than Innocence can bear: only Experience could read this rune. Horrified, the virgin Thel flies back to her native state.

Why should Thel have such a vision? Why should she suffer such horror?

Blake lived in a sentimental age when Nature was regarded as a pleasant menial who ministered gracefully to the life of man. Rousseau was preaching the Return to Nature and Marie Antoinette was keeping her court of Dresden shepherdesses. Nowadays we know all about the war of instinctive life, but in his steady gaze upon the fertilization of flowers Blake was a hundred years before his time. Whatever he might have thought of sex-instruction via botany, it is clear that he would not have sentimentalized the lesson by omitting to show that pollenization is often a haphazard event begotten of fierce instinctive strife. Thel was not enabled to regard the marriage bed with graceful equanimity because she had received instruction from the matron Clay. For Blake knew that what implies mortal life implies death. He knew that except a corn of wheat fall into the ground and die, it abided alone. He knew that youth cannot walk with single consciousness into the kingdom of imagination—that love implies supreme sacrifice and that without the recompensing consciousness only Imagination can give, sexuality is a soul-destroying waste of life. Experience is for Blake the grave of self. So when, in lonely singleness, Thel contemplates "her own grave-plot," she neither murders her own innocence, nor dons the deceitful cloak of modesty: she does not even brazen it out with a mask that hides the quivering and lacerated soul: she flies in terror, and by her flight, proclaims her perfect integrity.

How shall the unloved give themselves to experience? Unless this realm be entered through the gates of love, what can it be but a place of lonely horror, since only by love can we find Imagination, the redeemer, in the grave?

Thel is finally no human girl, but the soul itself at the moment of its separation from the innocence of Eden. That moment is the moment of "the Fall" which Blake identified with the coming of self-consciousness.

The Book of Thel is perhaps the most beautiful narrative poem ever written. It has a peculiar iridescent colour of its own perfectly suited to its theme. Its atmosphere is the atmosphere of spring sunrise. It tells a tale as plainly as if it were written in prose, yet it moves as on wings of gossamer with a lightness and poise that betoken perfect control. Take the following passage and note with what perfect sympathy the movement hesitates, pauses and mounts, like an incoming wave, to break at last in sheer abandon on the shore of pity:

> Dost thou, O little Cloud? I fear that I am not like thee,
> For I walk through the vales of Har, and smell the sweetest flowers,
> But I feed not the little flowers: I hear the warbling birds,
> But I feed not the warbling birds, they fly and seek their food;
> But Thel delights in these no more, because I fade away,

> And all shall say, 'without a use this shining woman liv'd,
> Or did she only live to be at death the food of worms?'

The measure of *Thel* is like the long breath the freshening air takes at dawn: its human figures seem to have been just breathed into existence. For sheer lyric beauty Blake never did anything lovelier: the grace and tenderness are beyond comparison exquisite and magical. Did he, I wonder, write it to console his childless wife?

In *The Book of Thel* Blake shows us the soul trembling on the threshold of experience. In *Visions of the Daughters of Albion*, Thel, who has become Oothoon, crosses the threshold.

Too literal a reading of this book has dulled its significance. The theme has dramatized itself with such force that literal interpretations have been read into it which obscure Blake's subtle meaning. Here as everywhere, Blake's concern is wholly with the life of the soul. Oothoon is the soul in Experience and not a particular woman suffering a particularly harrowing experience. The visions are Blake's visions, and Oothoon's story is not a tale of coarse outrage and desertion, but an account of what the soul suffers in mortal incarnation. Bromion and Theotormon are not the traditional husband and lover of the old triangle theme, but evocations of the soul: states through which the soul in its mortal journey is compelled to pass. The whole drama takes place on the stage of the soul, and to drag it from thence to the open market-place, is to debase its value and distort its characters.

The title page to *Thel* showed us the first act of this drama. There we saw Thel gazing with wonder and reproach upon the nuptials of the flowers, herself no actor in the scene, but an absorbed onlooker whose eyes were opening. The title page to the *Visions* illustrates the third act of the same drama. Here she occupies the centre of the picture. Her love expressed has awakened the terrors of the deep, and now she flies naked over the tempestuous Sea of Time and Space to escape from a wrath that emerges in flames from the clouds behind her. As she flies she looks back upon the nude figure of a man who reclines high upon the clouds. He regards her not, but only looks with hungry terror upon the flames of the abyss below him. The woman is

Oothoon. The bearded man is Bromion. The figure in the clouds is Theotormon.

> To find the Western path
> Right through the gates of wrath

Oothoon urges her way, and to mitigate the terror of her experience there is nothing but a rainbow—not the full completed bow, but the increasing arc climbing the sky—which symbolizes the promise that Imagination will yet redeem the soul from despair. The contrast between the two title pages gives us Blake's contrast between the Soul in Innocence and the Soul in Experience.

Oothoon we know, but who are Bromion and Theotormon?

The only way to read Blake is to read him from A to Z, For he is a progressive writer and his effects are cumulative. He worked like a spider throwing out the main lines of his web and then linking these together by a series of the most subtle connections. Once a vivid image occurred to him he seldom let it go. At its inception it is comparatively easy to recognize; but thenceforward he will apply it in a hundred contracted forms which are quite unrecognizable to those who have not seen the initial appearance. Take the flower, for example. The first flower mentioned in the *Songs of Innocence* is "The Blossom." Once we understand that the blossom is a symbol of love, then we shall find love symbolized throughout Blake as a garden in which the flowers are always symbols of human love. Blake was pre-eminently an expressionist in the sense that he was forever pushing forward toward fuller and more precise expression of what he perceived. He did not pause to present the same image in half a dozen different lights as more static poets have loved to do. He was an adventurer, and those who read him must follow him, or he is quickly lost to sight. The track is strewn with clues to the road he took, but unless we accept them he is soon lost on mountain tops that have ravines and impassable chasms beneath them.

In the present instance, Bromion and Theotormon are likely to remain unintelligible figures to anyone who has not read the preceding *Marriage of Heaven and Hell.* But if we have given that work worthy attention, we shall remember that Blake had much to say there about desire and restraint. In fact, if we turn to *plate 5* of *The Marriage of Heaven and Hell* we shall find in the opening sentences the characters of Bromion and Theotormon described in detail.

Title-Page of "Visions of the Daughters of Albion"

"Those who restrain desire do so because theirs is weak enough to be restrained; and the restrainer, or reason, usurps its place and governs the unwilling. And, being restrain'd, it by degrees becomes passive till it is only the shadow of desire."

Bromion is the Restrainer: Theotormon the Restrained, who by degrees becomes passive till he is only the Shadow of Desire.

Throughout the so-called Prophetic Books Blake's correspondences present intellectual difficulties which it would be foolish to deny; but whenever our sympathy and patience are sufficient to the task of recognizing these correspondences, the delicacy and precision of Blake's thought become evident. In the case of these three identities we see that by this method Blake has been able to identify and give a name to attributes of the soul which are perfectly recognizable, and hereafter immediately to be up called by their names in their exact significance, though they are essentially of such a character as almost to defy prose definition. They are attributes of consciousness, hitherto unnamed, that Blake saw as spiritual identities.

Oothoon is "the soul of sweet delight that can never be defiled." She is desire in its inherent purity. She is the soul in its incarnation. She is youth in perfect bud. She is the vindication of the senses. She is the means whereby the world is perpetually rejuvenated. Yet she is not the essential spirit. She is not Enitharmon. She is not the soul of poetry. Her love is the love of spontaneous self-expression, not of imaginative understanding. The soul of ideal aspiration is not the soul of all the world. Oothoon is the soul at a definite moment in its earthly history, wholly lovable, though her state is perhaps the most fleeting of all the states that make up the mortal life of man.

Bromion is the Restrainer. He is the embodiment of legal righteousness. He is man's passion for order in society. In the matter of sex, this passion for order has led him to prefer form to the life which creates form. Love outside the bonds of marriage is an offence to him, and where there is love he is ready to impose marriage, if need be against all human desire. He wants to fetter the soul in chains of logic

> And render that a lawless thing
> On which the soul expands its wing.

But Bromion is not Urizen. Urizen is tyrannous in the spiritual realm: Bromion rules in the social world of state and law. He cannot pine, as Urizen does, for spiritual bliss, for he belongs to an inferior hierarchy. He is Roman, not Greek law. His habitation would be nearer Temple Bar than Lambeth Palace. Bromion is, above all else, fear of the consequences—a fear that in degree has its cave in every mind.

Theotormon is "the Shadow of Desire"—desire that, by reason of external restraint, has become as the shadow to the living body. The living body in this case is Los, the representative on earth of the Poetic Genius, Los the Time-Spirit, poet and seer, whose desire in its essence is desire for God. Theotormon is desire in experience suffering from self-consciousness. He is no longer of the giant race. But desire is always desire. Blake's plummet drops sheer from heaven down to hell: he does not break his line to measure the abyss. Desire does not become a perversion by coming into touch with the senses. It is solely by his contact with Bromion that Theotormon is nullified. Theotormon is desire in restraint, in contrast to Oothoon who is desire in freedom. Theotormon stands for man in the present state of society, torn between the yea of the senses and the nay of doubting intellect—a creature of infinite longing, spiritually emaciated by his fears, who permits his energy to be dissipated by assenting to laws other than those of his own being. He is the soul of religious compromise, compromise which cannot escape cognizance of the body, but is compelled to strive against it because, never having had the spiritual vigour fully to accept the body, it is never able truly to transcend it.

But as Restraint and Fear have no existence apart from Desire, so, in this poem, Bromion and Theotormon have no existence apart from Oothoon. That neither is to be regarded as an objective personality, but that both are animating principles which achieve identity, is clear if we observe carefully the time and manner of their appearance.

The argument spoken by Oothoon states that she loved Theotormon. But essentially Theotormon is only the shadow of herself, the materialized form of her own aspirations. She is thus in love with her own ideal, and what better image could we have of a girl's first love? She hides "in Leutha's vale." Leutha, as we learn elsewhere, is "a daughter of Beulah," and Beulah being the realm of human love, Leutha stands for sex-attraction in the realm of experience. She plucks Leutha's flower (the plucking of the flower being the old symbol of sexual experience) and rises up from the vale, but the terrible thunders of Bromion destroy her virgin innocence.

When we come to the poem itself, neither Theotormon nor Bromion is mentioned until after the principal event, the plucking of the flower. As the whole poem is a description of the state that event gives rise to, their omission is highly significant. All that happens subsequently is consequent upon Oothoon's action, and the chief consequences are Theotormon and Bromion themselves. Blake wanted to dramatize the events that transpire within the soul itself; so Oothoon is presented as, of her own volition, plucking the flower. It is inconceivable that if Blake had wanted to write a drama of three persons, he should have omitted all mention of two of them until after the crucial action had taken place. Moreover, once the consequences of that act are fully apparent to Oothoon, Blake shows no further interest in Theotormon or Bromion as dramatic personalities. The stage is hers. They exist throughout only in relation to her. They are creatures of her environment and all the existence they have is subordinate to, and consequent upon, her action.

Visions of the Daughters of Albion is primarily Blake's passionate vindication of the inherent truth of the individual soul. Theotormon and Bromion generalize; but again and again Oothoon differentiates. All things are the same to Theotormon; for Oothoon everything has its own principle of being, its own law, its own individual identity. "One law for the Lion and Ox is oppression." Why? Because their instinctive activities being by nature opposite, obedience to a common law would destroy both types. Blake believed the purpose of creation to be the establishment of individual identities and whatever acted in opposition to that fundamental purpose was for him Satanic.

In a secondary degree the poem is a vindication of instinct. It is also an arraignment of man in his relations to woman. Inadequacy is written all over Theotormon. That inadequacy Blake particularly despised and years before had written in his notes on Lavater: "Let the men do their duty, and women will be such wonders. The female life lives from the light of the male. See a man's female dependents—you know the man."

Theotormon is the victim of his own weakness and a vacillation that destroys his character. Loved as the fulfillment of desire by a pure spirit, he is too weak to prevent the accomplishment of his own wishes from being annulled by an intellectual tyranny imposed upon him. Hence he remains "wretched Theotormon"—at once the prey of ungratified desire and fearful restraint. Therefore while the woman, passing through the terrors of experience, is able to achieve the imaginative height of

> Arise, you little glancing wings, and sing your infant joy!
> Arise, and drink your bliss, for everything that lives
> is holy!

he remains sitting.

> Upon the margin'd ocean conversing with shadows dire.

As was Thel, Oothoon is justified by her own integrity. Blake knew of no other holiness. Conformity, alike to good or evil, is abhorrent alike to divine and human love.

7
The Divine Imagination

There is no subject upon which clear thinking is rarer than the Imagination. As already suggested, the word itself in common parlance is made to do duty for all manner of ideas, some of them directly contrary to one another. We ask a man to 'use his imagination' and thereby imply that his thought is localized and insufficient. The next minute we speak of an idea as 'pure imagination' meaning this time that the idea is quite untrue. A jealous person is commonly described as a 'victim of his own imagination'; in the next breath we pay an individual the highest compliment by describing him as 'a man of imagination.'

The commonest criticism of Blake is that he was a man of unrestrained imagination, whereby it is implied, not that he was too fond of giving to airy nothings a local habitation, but more simply that he was the victim of aimless phantasy —a muddle-headed person without a sane sense of values. Similarly Imagination comes to be regarded as a faculty which, like a child's balloon, is harmless and pretty only so long as it is attached to the stout string of common sense. By the same means we arrive at the criticism which calls the painter of fauns and fairies 'very imaginative,' and the painter of mean streets and old women, 'realistic.'

Thus the word 'Imaginative' has no status. It is a complimentary or derogatory adjective according to the person who uses it. 'Reasonable' on the other hand has very proud status. To be called 'a reasonable man' is to be almost flattered; but when we think in terms of imagination, even 'man' has a way of disappearing, and the term is apt to become 'imaginative creature.' It may be a delicate compliment, but it remains delicate, and balances on the edge of dispraise.

What does all this signify? That "there is nothing either good or bad but thinking makes it so" is perhaps truer of the Imagination than anything else. As Imagination cannot be reasonably defined, each man's definition of it becomes the measure of himself. According to our imaginations is it unto us, and as with every other word of large significance, we raise or depress its value as our idea of it is great or small. But it is important to remember that the word has, and can have, no fixed significance.

While it has no fixed significance it has value, value that fluctuates. When Blake was born its value was very low, lower than it had been for centuries. Its value had increased by leaps and bounds before he died; but in general currency its worth was yet very far from what he himself attached to it, and although its value has been steadily increasing ever since, it still remains far below Blake's estimate, and it is still without status. We do not glory, as Blake would have done, in the description of himself as a poet of unrestrained imagination.

Before we decide that he was deluded it behaves us to find out, as far as we can, what Blake meant by Imagination.

Blake was a Christian. First and last, if not absolutely all the time, Blake was a Christian; and we do well to insist upon this fact because it colours all his ideas and most deeply his ideas upon Imagination. He has been called a mystic, and while we may admit the distinction, again we shall do well to remember that he never used it of himself. Blake believed his experiences were common in degree to all men; and while we may most profitably follow him along the pathway common to mystics, as Mr. Foster Damon has done so admirably, we begin to harbour demons of delusion if we think of this only as a strange and exclusive track which men with a perverse love of abstraction followed. It is all too easy to differentiate between great men and little and to behold the great like wandering stars whose significance to us is merely spectacular. By such processes systematized religions are made, which we conform to with our lips and use as Cerberus to our hearts. Blake, who called the spectacular God, Nobodaddy and The Human Abstract, and the spectacular Christ, a creeping Jesus, must not himself be turned into a strange phenomenon by mere classification. His mysticism is easily overemphasized.

But Blake was a Christian and a Bible Christian at that. He believed the Bible to be the inspired Word of God which contained between its covers the whole spiritual history of man. At the same time, unlike many of his day and a few surviving stalwarts of our own, he also believed Voltaire was a servant of God sent to destroy the literal interpretation of the Bible. "Why," says he in that letter to the Rev. Dr. Trusler which is of such ironic and yet profound interest, "is the Bible more entertaining and instructive than any other book? Is it not because they (the words) are addressed to the imagination, which is spiritual sensation, and but mediately to the understanding or reason?" And with these words, in this connection, we have a glimpse into what the Imagination meant to Blake.

"Spiritual sensation." That might mean many things to many people. It seems a turn of phrase that would be agreeable to the Spiritualist; but Blake, although at one time he dabbled amusedly with a harmless kind of spiritualism, was certainly not a spiritualist; nor did he mean to imply that open-mouthed credulity and faith in mediums was a means of grace. He doubtless knew all about the Witch of Endor, and the only ghost he ever conjured for himself gave him an experience in sensation which he would hardly have described as "spiritual."

Similarly, at the opposite pole, "spiritual sensation" is surely a phrase that would mean much to the Salvationist. Again we may take it that Blake did not mean to suggest spiritual sensationalism. By spiritual sensation he meant the power of sensing spiritual truth—of communicating with those spiritual powers which make and mould the material world—of penetrating the veils of custom, habit and tradition, and of seeing with extreme clarity the reality or essential form.

Is not this what every artist does? Gone forever is the day when it could be thought that the transference of appearances to canvas was art. If anything was wanting to remove that fond idea, the photographic camera supplied it. The most resolute artist, who paints what he sees and only what he sees, can only paint what he sees *as* he sees it; and if he is to be successful, nothing but his individual perception of the truth of the object he sees can save him from mere lineal journalism. What therefore he ultimately tries to portray is the truth he has perceived, and this, as modern art powerfully instructs us, *may* be far removed from the impression commonly derived from an object. So that in the final objective sense we may say that nothing—absolutely nothing—is true in itself: everything in the world is relative, and truth most relative of all, since it can never be known except by the union of subject and object. It is a matter of "spiritual sensation" or Imagination, and never of fact.

Where Blake was original was in breaking down compartmented ideas of the function of imagination. He announced not the religion of art, but of imagination. He redeemed imagination from its purely secular use and maintained that the power by which all art came into being was the very power which mediated God to man.

This is a tremendous idea and is at present far from being accepted. That the truth of nature can only be known by means of the imagination is believed by artists; but the exponents of religious doctrine are far from accepting the idea that it is precisely the same power by which any human soul has knowledge of spiritual truth. Religion is bound in the fetters of tradition and authority. Bibles and buildings, episcopacies and papal dignitaries are made the material residence of that which, by its nature, can have no material dwelling-place. To suggest that religion is purely a matter of imagination is to suggest the unthinkable, even today; but not until it has become a commonplace will art fructify with spiritual ideas, or religion blossom on the highway. Blake's work has the power and significance it has just because his traffic between heaven and earth was not impeded by the idea that religion was a spiritual and art a secular pursuit. It is here that he is truly prophetic. This is his marriage of heaven and hell, and when his idea is appreciated we may witness some such revival of spiritual consciousness as the world now so pathetically waits.

Blake perceived quite clearly that in the reasoning mind subject and object remain equal and opposite—that God is God and man is man and between them lays the chasm of infinity. The problem of consciousness he saw as the problem of bridging that chasm. This, reason could never do. By its nature it was restricted to the finite; but imagination, having no such limitation, could. Imagination could perceive "the infinite in everything," and in that moment of recognition discover that man is inseparable from God, and God not to be separated from man. Was not the power which bridged the gulf, the power of God himself, and if so, what was Irreligion but the relegation of this power to the rank of a mental amusement?

But imagination must have an object. Nothing comes out of nothing. The imagination that pursues art for its object pursues its own tail. "Art for art's sake" is the pursuit of imagination for imagination's sake. Its end is that perversion of imagination called phantasy, for as truth is relative, nothing exists for its own sake, not even the Imagination. Imagination is the dynamic power of faith, and the only true object of faith is God. Art flourishes or decays according to the adequacy of our ideas of God. When Keats said, "Beauty is truth, truth beauty," he perceived God in one of his attributes and the vision satisfied his imagination. When Blake wrote "The Divine Image" he perceived God as man and the vision filled him with worship. Art cannot be said to exist without a perception of God incarnate, and the more conscious that perception the more obviously religious the art. The revelation of what is human is the revelation of what is divine.

God Appears, and God is Light
To those poor Souls who dwell in Night,
But does a Human Form Display
To those who dwell in Realms of Day.

The characteristic of mystics is their application of imagination to theology. If knowledge and not action had been Blake's aim, he too could have been classed as a mystic and the definition would have embraced him. But Blake's chief value and interest lies in the fact that he was not content with theology. Blake was one with Jacob Boehme in his belief in the creative power of the Imagination and his consciousness that all true knowledge was knowledge of God; but Blake is distinctive in that he joins hands with Pope in the belief that the proper study of mankind is man. God apart from man (the mystic's constant pursuit) is Blake's idea of abstraction. Blake applied imagination not to theology, but to the soul of man, the soul which embraced the body, and there he saw God. "Human nature," he said "is the image of God." So strong was his conviction that God was not to be known apart from man that when he came to design the title for his greatest work, *Jerusalem*, he portrayed the spirit which emancipates souls from the slough of mortality as pointing to the words "Jesus only," and placed these words significantly in the crescent moon of human love. Blake had the mystics' conception of the use of imagination: where he differs essentially from them is in the purpose to which he applied it. The soul of man, and not God the divine essence, was his study. He declared the knowledge of God which is confined to mystical experience to be insufficient. God must be known, seen, felt, realized, loved and worshipped in every man. It is the Saviour in the likeness and similitude of his friend Los whom Albion recognizes in the redemptive moment of the last chapter of *Jerusalem*.

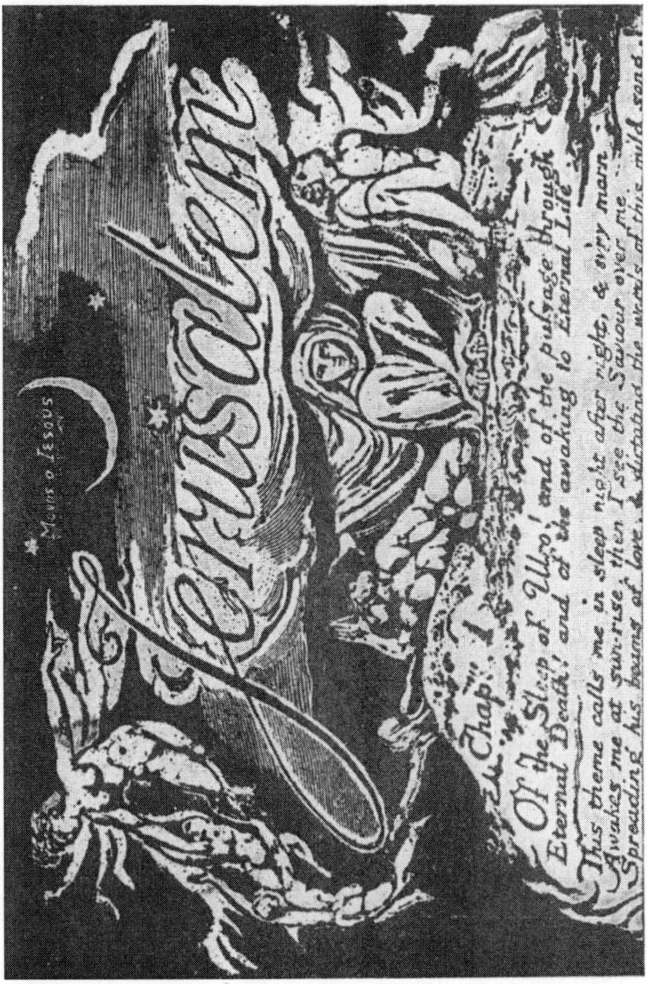

Chapter-Heading from "Jerusalem"

Blake had a poet's, not a mystic's, conception of the universe. In the early tractate, *All Religions are One*, where we see the germ of all Blake's ideas about the Imagination, we find that all things are derived from the Poetic Genius who is described as the true Man, the one source. Of this Poetic Genius, Jesus becomes the imaginative expression: "God descending according to the weakness of man." Hence, Jesus himself becomes the Divine Imagination, the Divine Vision and Fruition, the imaginative means whereby God is mediated to man. He becomes the archetype of all imagination. Correspondingly, the redemption of man being the creative work of God, man's work is redeemed by a similar process. It was cursed by being limited to knowledge in Eden. It is redeemed by partaking of the divine nature in being imaginative. Art is work redeemed from the curse, "In the sweat of thy face shalt thou eat bread."

Blake believed that man was encompassed about by God: that from the Fall he had shut himself up in the limitation of his five senses, but that Imagination, which was the divine expression of God, surrounded man like the invisible air, ever waiting for the act of faith whereby man cast himself upon the Divine Imagination and thus released himself from the bonds of mortality.

Imagination was the one way out of selfhood. Every other activity of the mind was a drawing into the selfhood of that which lay without, but in Imagination "Self was lost in the contemplation of faith and wonder at the Divine Mercy." It was man becoming as God in response to God's condescension in becoming as man. Consciously to experience this union with the divine, man had been given an individual body and had passed from essence to identity. Thus, Imagination was the divine communion of man with God: the only place from which reality was truly discernible, untroubled as reality was, when seen from the divine bosom, with the ephemera of nature. It was to make evident to those around him that this divine communion lay at hand to every human soul which had faith to abandon itself to the encompassing Divine Mercy that Blake wrote and illumined his passionate visions.

"This world of Imagination is the world of Eternity: it is the divine bosom into which we shall all go after the death of the Vegetated body. This World of Imagination is Infinite and Eternal, whereas the world of Generation, or Vegetation, is Finite and Temporal. There exist in that Eternal World the Permanent Realities of Every Thing which we see reflected in this Vegetable Glass of Nature. All Things are comprehended in their Eternal Forms in the divine body of the Saviour, the True Vine of Eternity, The Human Imagination."

To those who make it an accusation that Blake was a man of unrestrained imagination, Blake would have replied in the words he addressed to Byron: "Can a Poet doubt the Visions of Jehovah?" Imagination is either the true means of perception, or a delusive phantasy. The highest conception of form is either that seen by the imaginative eye, or that which may be mathematically demonstrated. Once Blake had identified Imagination with the Divine Image, it is easy to see that to doubt the essential truth of Imagination, and fancy that this divine power needed the assistance of those lesser powers which it held in fee, would have been for him something akin to blasphemous infidelity. "Man," he said in his *Notes to Lavater*, "is either the ark of God or a phantom of the earth and of the water." "Naturally, he is only a natural organ subject to Sense." "The Eternal Body of Man is The Imagination: that is God himself, The Divine Body, **ישע**, Jesus: we are his members."

The fundamental question which Blake's conception of the Imagination raises is this: Does Imagination comprehend Reason? In other words, in the practical, ordinary course of everyday life is Imagination a complete guide to conduct? Ought we to act reasonably and then add imagination as the cook adds spice to a dish; or supposing ourselves capable of acting with continuous imagination, shall we find our actions to have been supremely reasonable?

Similarly in art. Is Imagination a power sufficient, not merely to implant the idea of execution in the mind of the artist, to act as a lodestar to all his efforts, but is it also, of itself, capable of giving proportion and balance to the whole work of execution? Does Imagination need to be continually buttressed by reasonable ideas to prevent it from tapering into vacuity, or does it comprehend those reasonable ideas and render them not merely superfluous, but intrusive?

Blake believed the Imagination was sufficient for all things. His answer to our questionings would have been, 'According to your faith be it unto you. If you think Imagination insufficient, then for your Imagination will be insufficient, though what you add of Reason will never make up for what you lack of Imagination.' In his view, to act imaginatively was to seek first the Kingdom of God.

The question is fundamental because it is related to every sphere of human activity. Jesus was for Blake a symbol of the coming of Imagination to man. Innocence had ended with Adam. The Old Testament was the history of Man in Experience. With the advent of Jesus, man came to full consciousness, and this consciousness required of him the abrogation of the old law and imposed on him the new law—the law of imaginative understanding. The question (still unanswered) was, did the new law fulfil the old, or was the old law still necessary to buttress the new? Was the Christianity of Jesus good enough for practical purposes, or was it an ideal of perfection which the Church should hold before the eyes of men for admiring aspiration, while the real government of the world was continued on the sure foundation of the Ten Commandments? Blake saw the same cleavage between these two ideas as between Reason and Imagination. His history of the Law of the Ten Commandments was this:

> Against the Accuser's chief desire. . . .
> Jehovah's Finger wrote the Law

(thus giving to Evil a body that it might be destroyed)

> Then wept, then rose in zeal and awe
> And the dead corpse, from Sinai's heat,
> Buried beneath his Mercy Seat.

Even before the appearance of Jesus Jehovah had put Law beneath Mercy; but the faithless Church still clung to Law and Judgment unable to believe in the efficacy of Mercy. Whereat Blake cries:

> O, Christians! Christians! tell me why
> You rear it on your altars high?

Blake knew that the real reason was because Reason is so much easier than Imagination. "An eye for an eye and a tooth for a tooth" appeals to the reasoning faculty. It is a perfectly logical statement of justice; but great is the imagination and large the understanding of those who, without can't, love their enemies and bless those that curse them. Reasonably, this is impossible. It is the work of Imagination: the supreme work, for it argues the ability of one person to enter into and partake of the nature of his opposite. Thus it is that the supreme test of Imagination is the Forgiveness of Sins.

Blake saw that Imagination was the only way to achieve, not merely understanding, but happiness. And truly, nothing can despoil the happiness of the imaginative mind; for in so far as we live by imagination, we cease from egotism and live by enjoyment, instead of trying to live by possession. At self-consciousness we are brought to the realization of our solitude in the world and a sense of utter loneliness is the first fruit of self-consciousness. But this terrible experience, which awaits every sentient adolescent, is but the benediction of God whereby we know individuality. The happiness of Innocence passes for ever once we are conscious of our singleness in the world. But the experience of most young people is that, after a period of abysmal misery, they suddenly wake to find that by the exercise of imagination they are able to enter into the life of every living thing. The shell of self-consciousness cracks and they walk out, free of the universe, like the winged infant in the sixth plate of Blake's *Gates of Paradise.* They find that by imagination they have the power to be everything and everybody, and for a moment the whole world is enjoyed as the very image of God's glory. They see in a kind of heavenly mirage the truth of life. They become artists who can see the perfect picture but have no power to translate it in plastic terms. So they rush into experience, only to find the vision fade and themselves the victims of their own emotional powers. And these they must suffer until Imagination becomes actually incarnate and all their powers are made subservient to the only power that has a right to rule them.

It is thus we learn that only as we live by Imagination can we truly be said to live at all. For the nature of the soul is such that the soul can possess nothing: communion is its only life. Imagination is the means of communion—the soul's bread and wine. Without it the whole world acts in antagonism against us and the fight is against odds none can hope to overcome. But Imagination disarms us and transforms the attitude of the world. It brings us into living co-operation with every other form of life. We become what we behold and perceiving true forms we enjoy eternal life which no adversity of circumstance or chance of fortune can take away. We become inheritors of the world. The judge within is silenced, because he assumes now the throne of understanding and is no longer in the seat of the accuser.

And life ministers to us as we exercise our power of enjoying it. The hunger of self is appeased as we pass out of the circumscribed life of seeking self-satisfaction. We lose our lives to gain them. When the beauty of life perceived wins us over to participation in it, not for our own sakes or for the thought of any advantage, but for the sake of pure imaginative enjoyment, we wear the universe as a garment: we are converted and become as little children.

This is imaginative life. Everybody knows something of it, but we live it in miserable partiality usually because we try to live it in general terms on the strength of a single vision. The snare of organized religion is that it teaches this generalization, and the parson is a sentimentalist just because he tries to spread over the whole of life the joy of a moment that should have been surpassed as soon as it was experienced. He "binds to himself a joy" and we follow him just in so far as we lack faith to believe that every "minute particular" of life has its individual joy which it will momentarily yield to us if we are imaginatively awake.

Unlike the parson, the artist too often fancies that he can turn on his imagination as with a tap. To think this is to debase Imagination to the realm of fancy. It is to miss the universal vision and to make art the fruit of fleeting lynx-eyed perception, instead of continuous human vision. Such practice hardens the emotional values without which art loses its universality. Every phase of life must become imaginative if we would be deeply imaginative artists; for art reveals and is never deceived. There can be no imaginative peace in the work of an artist whose imagination is sporadic and fitful. Great art is not to be produced by response to intermittent states of imagination which we fancy we can evoke and retire from; but as a man is all the twenty-four hours of his day, so is his art. Our most intimate, our most casual personal relationships must be imaginative if we would know happiness or the service of art.

8
The Human Instinct

Great things are done when Men and Mountains meet. This is not done by Jostling in the Street.

So Blake noted in his manuscript book. For the good of his soul and the discipline of his patience every artist is compelled to a certain amount of jostling in the street. Bad artists thrive on it. Pickers and snatchers of unconsidered trifles, it is their means of livelihood, and in time they come to regard elbowing as the whole art of life. Good artists, on the other hand, reduce their jostling to a minimum; for while they realize that to make themselves impervious to environment is to become sterile and inhuman, they also know that the art of living implies discretion in the choice of environment, and since their job itself necessitates choice, they do not cultivate adventitious habits.

Blake was a sensitive, generous, sociable being whose heart found exercise with every social contact he made. "Open to joy and to delight wherever beauty appeared," he was only too ready to believe the best of every man, and in consequence was obliged to suffer many painful experiences before he learnt that the majority of his fellows lacked sufficient energy to feel his exuberance of good-will. With profound meaning he called Flaxman an angel, and had Flaxman been capable of responding with the same generous glow of affection he would have lived up to his reputation and literally been an angel: a Guardian Angel to a Prophet: no mean title to fame. But no doubt Flaxman's commonsense came to rescue him from so happy a fate. Unable to appreciate Blake's meaning or standpoint, he probably thought his friend wildly extravagant, and from such a judgment soon passed to the conclusion that Blake was sufficiently unbalanced to be called mad. So the potential swan lapsed into the ugly goose, and Blake learned a sad lesson.

There is the potential swan in every human gosling. In the "the Dark Lady," in Fanny Brawne, in Harriet Westbrook, in William Godwin, in Lord Byron, in William Hayley, ay, even in Robert Hartley Cromek, and genius breaks its heart in the effort to encourage the wild swan to grow. We do the highest powers of life a mighty wrong if, with the half-closed eyes of prudence, we see such efforts only as pitiful waste. Unbelief in the power of human beauty is the most fruitful cause of waste—waste that does not follow unsought crucifixion, which has ever been fruitful of the highest beauty. And you never can tell. Blake loved the gardener's daughter. It is customary to think of her as one of the uncrowned saints of literature; but without wishing to rob her of her candles, we divorce life from reality if we do not remember that she was married to a man of faith who could see the world in a grain of sand and believe that Cromek meant honestly. His wife was perhaps the greatest triumph of Blake's faith, and the constructive value of imagination is beautifully illustrated by his faith in her and her responsive faith in him.

But "jostling in the street"? No. There never was a man less fitted for the occupation. Besides, Blake had met his mountain. That mountain was the Christian Religion.

When Blake had written the *Songs of Innocence* he found himself committed to the soul of man for his study, and even supposing he had been terrified at the infinite prospect which opened before his eyes as he looked out upon the human soul, he could not have gone back and amused himself with art in the fashionable manner of his contemporaries. For one characteristic he possessed which will hardly be denied to him by his keenest detractor, and that was thoroughness. He was so whole-hearted that he simply lacked the ability to turn back from any path that the pursuit of his genius had led him to. And pondering on the human soul, almost the first object that met his gaze must have been the great mountain of systematized thought on the same subject enshrined in the Christian Religion.

That mountain meets us all—at least, organized religion in one form or another confronts every child more truly than Gilbert's choice of politics. As every child is naturally born into a family, so every man is spiritually born into a church. Whether it has a dome, or a spire, a belief or a disbelief matters little; the fact that it is our traditional lot is what counts. For just as the child has to release itself from parental bonds to become a man, so the human soul has to release itself from spiritual bonds to achieve identity. And just as it is necessary for a young man to extricate himself from the ties of his family before making affectional ties of his own, so is it necessary for a human soul to extricate itself from the spiritual ties of its traditional church if it is ever to form ties which are truly of its own making. We cannot inherit religion. We cannot purchase it second-hand. It is not to be had for the asking, either ready-made or to measure. Every soul has to make its own garment. The insistent demand of every soul is that it should have its own religion, and human souls are great according to the magnitude of the demand and the ability to respond to it.

> I must create a system or be enslav'd by another man's.
> I will not reason and compare, my business is to create.

How delightful to meet a man who could acknowledge so simply the demands of his own soul! And who would have thought that such forcible confession of the simple truth that spiritually, as naturally, we must grow up and express our individuality or die, could have been translated into the announcement of another quack religion? But so it has been, and panic-stricken members of one flock or another have been gravely concerned either to prove that Blake's religion was or was not theirs, or that it was not religion at all but merely one of the ancient heresies revived. The passionate pigeon-holers must be left to reason and compare as they will. Meantime, the business of individuals will remain—to create, each after his own order, a body of thought for his own religious faith.

From the *Songs of Innocence* to *The Ghost of Abel*, Blake's work may be described as one continuous effort to restate what he believed to be the truth of the Christian Religion. Let such a notice stand as a warning to those who are satisfied that no such restatement is necessary. Blake is not for them. And why should the satisfied concern themselves with the efforts of the dissatisfied? Let the orthodox preach orthodoxy till they are tired of sound and desire understanding.

Blake left the parental roof the day he walked out of a Swedenborgian Church for the last time. Probably he never needed to be delivered from the literalism of orthodoxy.

> The Good are attracted by Men's perceptions
> And think not for themselves,

he wrote, but the day when he did not think for himself is unrecorded. Swedenborg had been welcomed as a haven from the literalism that dominated every other form of Christian Religion. At least Swedenborg did not confound imagination with insanity, and a powerful mind thinking for itself was just the harbour young Blake needed to give him time to rig out his own adventurous ship. But the young thinker soon found the old one insufficient. Swedenborg closed up the mouth of the harbour with the bar of Predestination. So Blake set sail, burst the bar and took to the open waters.

Like all the Churches, Swedenborg had a useless Hell: a place of vague unpleasantness where unruly passions tortured one Another. According to Blake's thinking this Hell knocked the bottom out of every system of intelligent thought. It was an abyss that opened beneath every action. It was also the home of human passion, and this young man knew himself well enough to know that all his actions were passionate. The whole world seemed to live in imminent fear of toppling into this bottomless abyss, an abyss where passion turned to wrath.

Above lay the virgin Heaven, stainless, spotless, but sterile. For by contrast Heaven appeared as the eternal home of negation: the region where evil never came, only because desire was never awakened. And Swedenborg taught that man should live with his face to the sky, ever aspiring to the void, ever denying the passion which alone could give worth to any action. Such a doctrine tore the passionate young Blake in two. How could man live poised between immaculate complacence and useless wrath? What sort of a soul was it that could rest in the contemplation of either? And if between these eternal symbols of good and evil the soul practised evasion, what hope could there ever be of its regaining lost integrity?

Blake suddenly saw these two great contraries as complementary. So he joined them in holy wedlock and wrote *The Marriage of Heaven and Hell.* He solved the mystery in himself. Heaven, the realm of Hope, lay before him. Hell, the region of Fear, lay behind. Vision was the synchronization of the two. The meeting of hope and fear was vision, and vision was the perception of identity itself.

The spiritual life descended and was from Heaven. The instinctive life ascended and was from Hell. As the plant had its roots in the ground while its shoots aspired towards the sky, so man, rooted in Hell, aspired to Heaven and flowered upon Earth. Life instead of being, as the Churches taught, the opportunity for exercising moral virtue or goodness, and thus showing that man was one with the Divine Essence, was the means by which man achieved conscious individual identity, which identity had nothing to do with good or evil, being an eternal reality awaiting human recognition. This principle of identity held good for all things. Sheep and goats, angels and devils, good men and evil men, cunning and courageous, prolific and devourers—all were necessary to human existence, for without contraries human life was unthinkable. Mortality was not the opportunity for man's pathetic effort towards eternal sameness, but was Immortality made visible: distinction and difference revealed so that every living thing might exhibit its eternal form, and by showing its eternal form reveal its individual holiness.

Thus at one bound Blake released himself from the toils of morality and surpassed, not only Swedenborg, but his old friend the moralist Lavater. Henceforth Good and Evil ceased to be the essential differences; the essential differences lay deeper and were not to be resisted, being as necessary to human life as the contrary acts of respiration were to the body.

For a moment Blake rejoiced in the sense of freedom that always ensues when we have put behind us restraints not of our own making, and all restraint seems to be the work of the devil. But of course Blake had not solved the insoluble problem of duality: he had only raised the standard. The moment we cease to conform to external discipline, in that moment life imposes upon us the necessity of conforming to a far more rigorous discipline—the self-discipline upon which true form depends. Blake passed from the discipline of good and evil to the far more rigorous discipline of imaginative or unimaginative life, and having written the enfranchising *Marriage of Heaven and Hell*, he was soon to find, in tears of repentance, that the very means whereby we achieve spiritual enfranchisement quickly turns to pride unless we pass from vision to vision. God made duality that man might know the supreme joy of balance in the ecstasy of creation; but when vision fades and we eat in pride the fruits of vision, fancying that we have attained, we turn our joy to sorrow. In his moment of insight Blake enfranchised the human body as a part of the human soul; but unless I misinterpret the tears of Urizen in the Fifth Night of *Vala,* the body, in Blake's idea, assumed a pride in its own glory during the years that intervened, and taught Blake that Gods may "combine against Man setting their dominion above The Human Form Divine," and that none is so ready to do this as a rightly-enfranchised instinct.

But now Blake saw very clearly what has since been demonstrated psychologically, that the repression of energy only changes its shape.

How did this discovery appear in the light of Christian dogma?

The Christianity that was based upon the Ten Commandments appeared to exist chiefly to exercise this restraint upon human instinct. It put division between the soul and body and by this putting asunder attempted to frustrate the essential purpose of mortal life which was the manifestation of the soul in form. It separated human life from the continuous life of Eternity by making moral perfection, which was only possible to God as essence, the ideal of human life; the true ideal being the complete revelation of individual identity. In consequence it necessarily destroyed the whole purpose of incarnation. God was removed from earth and transplanted to the abstract heaven, and Jesus, instead of being the Incarnate Word, became merely an ideal historical character.

Blake regarded the Christianity of his day as the spiritual atavism Jesus came to destroy. It was the worship of God as light, a worship which Blake indicates in "The Little Black Boy" as natural and right to man in the childhood of the race, but atavistic and wrong to those who lived in the imaginative manhood of the race. The Divine Image a human form displayed. Even the Little Black Boy, living in the childhood of the race as he is, learns that he is put on earth a little space not only that he may learn to bear the beams of love, but that when he has done this, it may be for the express purpose of shading his white brother: of being "like him" and thus discovering the Divine Image in a human form.

Blake saw the crux of the whole matter lay in the denial of spiritual purpose to instinctive life. So *The Marriage* resolves itself into a justification of instinct. Not the restraint, but the imaginative redemption of instinct is the purpose of experience; for when this is complete, not only will the five senses appear as "inlets of soul," but the cherub with his flaming sword will leave his guard at the Tree of Life and everything will appear as it is, infinite and holy. Everything that lives is holy, for everything possesses within itself its own sacred law of life, a law that can only be contravened by the imposition of any external law.

Blake's theme was the soul. It was natural therefore that the purpose of human instinct to the soul should be a subject of consuming interest to him. Instinct is that which brings the spiritual into the realm of the material. It is therefore primarily that which divides man from God. Blake saw it in the image of Lucifer and his fall from heaven, and in the image of Prometheus who stole the sacred fire. His own symbol for human instinct is Ore, who first appears unnamed in that fire-barred gate of symbolism with which Blake concludes *The Marriage—A Song of Liberty.*

The *Song* contains in epitome the myth which Blake expands in many subsequent prophetic books. Most unfortunately its connection with *The Marriage* has been severed for the past twenty years by Blake's editors who have treated it *as* if it were a separate poem. Ignorance of the poem's meaning can be the only excuse for this; but although unfortunate, that ignorance will certainly be condoned by every reader on his first approach to this extraordinarily abstruse piece of Work. Blake took to his wings and this time at one bound soared straight out of sight. To the unprepared reader nothing could be more disconcerting; but once again, before we bring up the old charge of willful obscurity we must remember, that in the use of symbols here, Blake was freeing himself from the bonds of prosaic argument which he must have felt had long detained and impeded him.

The symbols may impede us, but they were wings to him: they were his identifications of spiritual states which, so far as he was concerned, were released from disguise by being permitted to show themselves in direct characterization.

Blake was professedly writing "Visions of Eternity." From this standpoint a thousand years may be as one day: the historical sequence of Time may be telescoped at will. Since all is eternally existent, we may pass up and down the ranks of Time quick as thought can fly, selecting from the events of Time, without reference to date or duration, just those episodes which are relevant to the image to be created. The characters and episodes will be chosen not from any propinquity in Time, but solely for their spiritual, and therefore eternal, significance.

Just as an illustration of Blake's practice in this way, we may take the line from *The Four Zoos*, Night II:

> Reuben slept on Penmaenmawr and Levi slept on
> Snowdon.

Reasonably speaking, the sentence is, of course, absurd; but neglecting all thought of the date of Reuben's birth and the impossibility of his appearance of a Welsh mountain, we can associate Reuben biblically with a particular state of wickedness, and a mountain is pretty obviously a high place. So we shall understand that "spiritual wickedness" has become apparent "in high places" and those high places, being in the northwest of the land of Albion, will symbolize for us the spiritual enslavement of Albion's body—the north being the realm of the spirit, and the west being symbolic both of freedom and of the body.

If the reader asks what is to be gained by all this, the answer is: an economy and concentration of meaning otherwise impossible, giving a content which cannot be fully presented by the longest and most detailed prose exposition.

The Marriage of Heaven and Hell is Blake's book of emancipation. It treats successively of his own spiritual liberation: the freedom of Instinct: the emancipation of man from the fetters of moral law: the release from priesthood and its traditions: the soul's escape at the end of Time from the limitation of the five senses, and the freedom of inspiration from the bondage of reason. *A Song of Liberty* tells the same story from the standpoint of Eternity. Instinct is a child of the eternal spirit in its creative function. It is rejected in jealousy by the traditional guardian of the Golden Age and falls to earth as fire. Its rejection, however, involves the power that rejects it and he, too, falls with all his hosts to be buried in ruins of spiritual enslavement. Fallen, and fearful of the new-born power he has rejected, he promulgates his Law of Ten Commandments. But Instinct rises as inevitably as the sun and stamps the Law to dust.

America is really nothing but a fuller history of the same events. It is simply an expanded *Song of Liberty* with more particular adaptation to the historical events of Blake's own day. Intrinsically it has almost nothing to do with them: the actual events were symbolic of a warfare that was eternal in its nature. In *Europe* we find a still fuller history of Orc; and in *The Four Zoas* the theme receives its fullest treatment where Blake, narrating events that took place ages before the birth of Adam, shows how the division of the spiritual man, in his four phases of humanity, took place before creation was ready to receive this "howling terror," the Human Instinct. There we see its crucifixion by its spiritual parents: its consequent adhesion to the world of matter: its defiance of traditional religion and its final consummation and extinction before the resurrection of the eternal man to the Last Judgment. "Orc is generated Luvah," that is, Love in the act of generation, a state dependent upon mortal existence.

In the four-fold Eternal Man it has no place; for in the world of Eternity its work of determining human individuality is done and Instinct is wholly superseded by Imagination. In the life that is beyond mortality the spiritual purpose of instinctive life has been completed.

9
The Beams of Love

If one were asked to give in A phrase a clue to the whole of Blake's work, one could hardly do better than quote the sentence from "The Little Black Boy,"

And we are put on earth a little space
That we may learn to bear the beams of love.

It contains the idea that man is an eternal spirit definitely put upon this earth. It suggests that the world from which he comes is a place of such intense light that he needs the shade of mortality to be able to bear its beams, thereby inferring that the ultimate joy of man is the appreciation and love of God. It puts the period of human life into Blake's proportion as "a little space," and, while it assumes that life itself is a discipline, it declares that, that discipline has the most beneficent purpose we can imagine, since to be as fully as possible the recipient of love is the natural desire of every human heart.

The lines are finely characteristic of Blake in that, while they are full of the tenderest sentiment, they do not show the least sign of toppling over into sentimentality. They are a profound statement of spiritual truth expressed with the maximum of simplicity and human feeling. Above all, they seem to me to succeed in *placing* the emotion of love, and to be able to do that is perhaps the last word of human wisdom.

In our attitude to love we all stand naked, shamelessly revealed for what we are and where- unto we have attained. Love admits of no disguise. If you would conceal yourself do not speak of love; for the most subtle disguise is the most apparent means of self-revelation. Shakespeare is to be measured by his attitude to love. *Romeo and Juliet*, *Antony and Cleopatra*, *Timon of Athens*, *Julius Caesar*, indeed every single play of Shakespeare might be made a touchstone of Shakespeare's attitude to human love and seen as illustrative of his idea of the purpose and place love had in human existence. Among other reasons, Shakespeare is Shakespeare because he knew the geography of the human heart from the equator to the poles, and because he knew, moreover, that while the human frame depends upon its central pumping-station, the heart does not exist to show its blood, but to enable the human form to live in sentient relationships. Love was to Shakespeare the means of life and not, as it is in the hands of the second-rate novelist, the end.

Blake too is to be measured by his attitude to love. Indeed, he invites that estimate with a frankness that is startling; for he never seriously adopts the attitude of humour—that short cut to synthesis so dear to the mind that baulks sublimity. He is the most intimate of the poets. His poems are really love passages where the disguises of behaviour are thrown off and beauty is revealed by the uttermost candour. His passionate desire for spiritual freedom leaves him without a rag of disguise to conceal weakness that would pass unnoticed had he elected to appear in any traditional form. Had he restricted his canvas to man in society, as Shakespeare did, or to man as distinct from God, as Milton did, or to man in his relation to Nature, as Wordsworth did, he would have been a far less challenging author, far more easily acceptable, because he would have presented us with a portion of that externality which is acceptable to all. As it is, his mirror ultimately presents us with the image of his own soul, naked and unashamed: a spectacle of sublime wonder and infinite beauty, or of pitiable and mortal weakness, according to the love and sympathy of the beholder. It is ultimately not by precept or exposition—not by the clearest enunciation of principles that were essential to his own understanding, that Blake conveys his unique gift; but, standing in all the simple majesty of a soul in the adoration of truth, he becomes in measure transformed into the likeness of what he beholds and in his own person justifies the ways of God to man. This is divine humility, or outrageous pride, again according to our love and sympathy.

But Blake's theme determined his method for him. Simplicity is the language of the soul: it cannot speak without candour. Humour is impossible to the soul, for it cannot make proportionate the Infinite. What the soul has to say about love will not be polite, because politeness is an equivocal consideration, and such considerations the soul literally cannot make. 'Let us therefore change the subject,' say those to whom behaviour is the essence of life. But Blake was not of them. He had no drawing-room in his house of life. There were only two rooms in his apartment at Fountain Court, and one of them was both bedroom and workshop, a significant association.

Blake had not finished the *Songs of Innocence* before he found that man was a dual creature with contrary principles embedded in his nature. Instinct and Imagination warred within him and presented attitudes to life which were both opposite and antagonistic. There they were, the Lamb and the Tiger, and much as the Lamb might be loved and consecrated, the Tiger made short work of it in this world. Of course the contrast was spurred by reasonable people who went amiably about their ways and never troubled to wonder if there could be any spiritual meaning behind the fact that black was black and white. Religion appeared to uphold the Lamb; but as far as the Tiger was concerned, religion bade men hide their eyes in the sand with the ostrich. This did not satisfy Blake, who held with Thomas Hardy:

> If way to the Better there be, it exacts a full look
> at the Worst.

So he looked at the Tiger with a gaze that did not flinch. He looked on human love with the same eyes and there he saw

> Love seeketh not Itself to please
> Nor for itself hath any care,
> But for another gives its ease
> And builds a Heaven in Hell's despair,

and then he also saw that it is equally true

> Love seeketh only Self to please
> To bind another to Its delight
> Joys in another's loss of ease
> And builds a Hell in Heaven's despite.

Kind, religiously-minded critics of Blake have unwittingly attempted to destroy this poem by explaining that in the second of these verses Blake, of course, did not mean Love, but Lust.

Certain it is that if he did, the poem was not worth writing; for so worded it states a truism. Blake, however, said Love, and Love he meant.

Here are contraries that are true and must remain coexistent. They are reverse and obverse faces of the same medal. Without self-pleasing there can be no love. "The lineaments of gratified desire" can never be seen without the love that seeketh only self to please? Invertebrate sentimental self-negation is the destiny of those who think love can be comprehended by the love that seeketh not itself to please. Divided from its contrary, such love inevitably leads to hypocrisy— the hypocrisy that has made modern Christianity a disease.

> Let man wear the fell of the lion, woman the fleece of
> the sheep.

Love that seeks not its own can only be the fulfillment of love that seeks naught but its own; and this fulfillment can only be achieved through the power of imagination. Love is a process of becoming one, and the fulfillment of two desires is necessary to that end. In so far as that unity is incomplete (as incomplete it must be while we remain in individual bodies) individual and separate desires exist to be gratified in the activity of love.

But, on the contrary, selfishness that leads to self-loathing is the fate of those who believe that love can be comprehended by the love that seeketh only self to please? In so far as love has achieved unity and is complete, the lover seeks only the joy of the beloved; for having, by imagination, become the beloved, two desires become identical. Yet we cannot give unless we possess. Self-assertion is essential to individuality, and until we have reached individuality through self- assertion, imagination cannot function. Love without desire is sterile; but love is redeemed from greed by imagination. That is the miracle. But those who will have love to be *either* selfishness *or* self-denial cannot know love. For it is neither. It is at once self-expression and atonement through imagination, and thus the prototype of all man's highest activity.

In Blake's conception duality is an inherent condition of human life; for at birth man is separated from God-as-essence in order that man may have consciousness of individual life. The means whereby individual life comes to birth is instinct. The means whereby it attains consciousness is imagination. Instinct is the primary condition of mortal life: it is the separating power whereby the particles of the stream of life are to be distinguished from the stream itself; therefore, the assertion of instinct is essential to individuality. To deny instinct is to deny individual life and attempt the merging of unique individual consciousness in a general consciousness of that God from whom man was separated at birth for a distinct and specific reason. This specific purpose Blake describes as

> to bring Albion again
> With Luvah into light eternal in his eternal day;

but the denial of instinct creates an abstract God and destroys the hope of individual perception. This was to Blake perversion against which he contended with all his vigour from the day he wrote *The Marriage of Heaven and Hell* to the end of his life.

Blake's acceptance of instinct did not, however, blind him, as it blinded Nietzsche to the ultimate purpose of human life. This purpose Blake conceived of as the reunion of man with God, not by any retrogressive step in the direction of Innocence, involving the denial of instinct, but in full acceptance of instinct, by the redemption of instinct through the power of Imagination. That was Blake's conception of the Christian Religion. The object of creation was not that the soul should again be absorbed in the essence of God, but that, in the biblical phrase, the soul should return to the bosom of God individualized as the bride of the Lamb. Man, Blake held, was never made God-like by being less than man, and on the other hand, by "attempting to be more than man we become less."

Thus Blake parts company for ever with those who live in fear of instinct, just as he parts company with those who believe that the expression of instinct is the whole purpose of life. As Desire is necessary that Reason may have ideas to build on, so Instinct is essential that Imagination may have a soul to save.

In *Visions of the Daughters of Albion*, Blake made his most passionate assertion of the rights of instinct, and there the persistent cry of Oothoon is that individuality is its own justification. The wisdom of instinct is illustrated by the actions of the chicken, the pigeon, the bee, the mouse, and the frog. The distinctive purpose of instinct is shown by comparisons between the instincts of different animals. That it is impossible for joy to express itself through conformity is shown by the differing experiences which give pleasure to different kinds of men. The fearful effects of imposed law upon instinct are described with a penetrative particularity that sends a shudder through the mind. Blake saw that without freedom of choice the soul could never know individuality: that love which was bound by the fetter of a single consideration, other than that of its object, was a form of self-love preventing the soul from its true incarnation. The poem is youth's passionate plea for absolute freedom of instinct in order that choice may be the individual assertion of the soul.

Because of his frank and wholehearted acceptance of instinct, Blake has been dubbed an advocate of "free love."

It was inevitable that it should be so, and need not be regretted. Popular ideas of greatness inevitably suffer from inadequacy. No doubt the mole thinks that the eagle moves without circumspection; and if so, we need not therefore blame the mole or the eagle. "Free love" is a loose phrase that has happily passed out of general currency among educated people because it came to mean anything and therefore nothing. Its literal alternative is "bound love," and bound love is a contradiction in terms. When the phrase had currency it used to denote a want of spiritual integrity and a personal abandon for the sake of sense gratification. "Free love" meant an indiscriminate, and therefore superficial, planting of the affections, its very virtue consisting in the weakness of its roots and the ease with which they might be transferred capriciously to more pleasure-yielding soil.

Such characteristics hardly consort with the elements of Blake's nature. It is fabled that he once wished to add a concubine to his household. Forty concubines could not have so altered the nature of Blake as to make him a superficial lover. The prophet of imagination was the least likely of all poets to be beguiled by vagrant fancy. Freedom he adored and demanded as the soul's inherent right; but the freedom he sought and found was a condition of spiritual activity, not of laxity such as dalliance might wander into. Blake's idea of passion as a heightened and enlarged state of the soul forbids the notion that he could be the advocate of the weak and craving desire for spiritual props. They do not "learn to bear the beams of love" whose love is the flickering light of will-o'-the-wisp. The difference between the free choice of the soul and the beguiling of the senses is the difference between love of God and acceptance of the serpent's gift, and Blake drew the line between them sharp and clear. Not to observe that line is to read Blake upside down, or 'black' where he wrote 'white.'

This has literally happened in regard to such a passage as that in *The Marriage of Heaven and Hell* where Blake says that the consummation of the whole creation "will come to pass by an improvement of sensual enjoyment." The passage has been interpreted to mean that Blake thought a general riot of the senses was a desirable consummation. The contrary is his meaning. The "improvement" he prophesies first waits upon the expulsion of "the notion that man has a body distinct from his soul," and apparently Blake gives another four thousand odd years for the penetration of this notion into the consciousness of man. Again, a "sensual enjoyment" which is dependent upon the recognition of body as "a portion of Soul," is obviously the antithesis of that sensuality which is essentially soulless. A "sensual enjoyment" which makes the whole creation "appear infinite and holy," must be very unlike the Hell of "being shut up in corporeal desires." Blake is, of course, speaking of the liberation of the body from the confines of contracted senses, and not the handing over of the soul to the tormenting confines of sensuality—of spiritual enfranchisement, not of slavery to finite senses.

So long as the soul is regarded as so much precious burden which the body as an ass is called upon to bear, the fate of the soul in this world will be that of those travelers in the fable who ended their journey by carrying the beast that should have borne them. But when the senses (and Blake speaks of all five and not only of the sense of touch, which is sex) are enjoyed as "inlets of soul"—avenues through which spiritual perceptions can be made, then matter will no longer hamper the soul, but the doors of perception being also cleansed, everything will appear as it is, infinite. "The cloud will vanish" when man perceives that the senses are not blind alleys of pleasure, but avenues of the soul enabling him to "see small portions of the eternal world that ever growth" and "to pass out what time he please." And this is the "improvement of sensual enjoyment" of which Blake speaks.

More specifically he clearly intended to indicate his belief that sexual intercourse, prompted and sustained by imagination, was the redemption of Eden itself. It was an eating of the Tree of Life whereby the disparate creation of male and female was "consumed" and man and woman were again united into one being. For Blake believed that the separation of sex was a mortal condition which would be surpassed in eternity where there was neither marrying nor giving in marriage. But he not only believed that sexual intercourse could be a foretaste of eternal joy; he believed that men and women had "spectrous" as well as "emanative" bodies; bodies that were "opake" as well as bodies that were "translucent"; and full well he knew that if the sexes met in spectrous opacity, closing their eyes to imaginative perception, then the senses, instead of being enlarged and purified by sensual enjoyment, were stultified and darkened, and souls instead of passing from Beulah, the land of love, into Eternity, the realm of vision, descended into Ulro, the world where matter held the soul in chains of sleep.

Blake's "sensual enjoyment" is not the pleasure but the joy of the senses, which released from the deathly confinement of being ends in themselves, show themselves to be what they truly are—means of spiritual apprehension. By so much as sexual intercourse is this, it is "infinite and holy"; by so much as it is less than this, it is "finite and corrupt."

None the less let no one think that Blake during all the seventy years of his life was a paragon of spiritual wisdom who never fell into the pit which the unredeemed instinct digs for the souls of men. There are clear indications to the contrary. Blake suffered as we all suffer. And let it be remembered, youth's assumption of instinctive freedom is youth's inalienable prerogative which we deny only to his lasting hurt. To taste, to touch, and to try is the way of experience, and none can know of imagination who has not tasted the cup of experience. Enamoured of his instinctive freedom, the youth of Blake's seventh illustration to *The Gates of Paradise* pursues the joys of sex without regard to personality. This is a state through 'which the unimpeded soul will quickly pass unless gross and enslaving notions of fidelity are imposed upon it. No constraint is needful to the soul once it has perceived imaginative reality in the face of another, nor need we impose our statute of limitations upon the number of such realities which any soul may perceive. Love becomes a sacrament to those who have seen the eternal form of the beloved; but a terrible fear of spiritual vagrancy, utterly foreign to the true nature of the soul, makes marriage a legal institution and love the most mistrusted power in the world.

Why is this? Is it not because Sex in the realm of Instinct has assumed to itself a finality akin to that which Reason assumed in the realm of Intellect? Blake thought so and wrote *The Four Zoas* to show how this happened.

At the close of his prose argument in *The Marriage of Heaven and Hell* he promised the world *The Bible of Hell.* As Blake usually kept his promises, it was assumed for a long time that he wrote such a book and that since it had vanished, it was probably burnt by Tatham. Almost certainly we may say this is not what happened. For on the back of an uncoloured drawing representing "A Naked Man touching a Ram as he recedes," Blake wrote the words in title-page form: "The Bible of Hell, in Nocturnal Visions collected. Vol. I. Lambeth." Blake lived at Lambeth from 1793 to 1800, and during that time was commissioned to illustrate, and made an immense number of drawings and engravings for another book of nocturnal visions, Edward Young's "Night Thoughts." The original title-page of *The Four Zoas* reads "Vala or The Death and Judgment of the Ancient Man. A Dream of Nine Nights by William Blake, 1797." From this we may pretty safely infer that the second title-page was an amended form of the first, and that *Veda* (afterwards again renamed *The Four Zoas)* is Blake's revised version of *The Bible of Hell.*

A study of the work confirms this belief. We should expect a Bible of Hell by Blake to be a survey of the spiritual history of man similar to that which the Hebrew and Greek Bible presents, but viewed, not from the standpoint of spiritual perfection, but from the standpoint of instinctive energy. This is just what we have in *The Four Zoas.*

The task was gigantic: the scale great as *The Divine Comedy*, and far greater than *Paradise Lost* which was essentially an epic rendering of events exactly as narrated in the Book of Genesis, though illuminated by Milton's learning and expanded by his sublime thought. Blake had no historical skeleton to clothe with flesh, but had himself to create the historical structure of his epic, and it is little to be wondered that he never succeeded in doing this to his complete satisfaction. *The Four Zoas* was never finally revised and Blake apparently did not begin to engrave it.

Why he never finished his revision of it is a nice question that leaves plenty of room for surmise and show of personal predilection. Very possibly he reluctantly came to the conclusion that in the present state of society it would be impossible to reproduce, without offence, illustrations of so frankly sexual a character as those that decorated this poem; and as there was no separation in Blake's mind between the illustrations he gave to a poem and the poem itself, this consideration alone would have sufficed to stay his hand. Then, I believe he was actively occupied with the MS. from about 1795 to 1803, the main portion of the work being written at Felpham. These were turbulent years in his life, full of painful impressions and vivid alternations of feeling. Work composed in a period of storm is difficult to rehandle in a period of subsequent calm, and it seems a natural surmise that Blake, having much else on hand, should decide in favour of the composition of another epic more suited to his older genius, rather than the cold rehandling of what had been written in the heat of the day.

In any case, *The Four Zoas* is, after *Jerusalem*, the most important of Blake's writings, and in the present state of our understanding of the prophetic works, in many respects the most valuable of them. It is simpler, younger, more vivid and continuous in its narrative than either *Milton* or *Jerusalem*., and therefore (after Night I) much more easily readable. Whether Blake intended it for the public or not is an idle question that might with equal irrelevance be asked of *Tiriel, The French Revolution*, the whole contents of the so-called Rossetti MS. and the poems of the Pickering MS. What is certain is that Blake cherished the manuscript of *The Four Zoas* for a quarter of a century and then, to ensure it safe keeping after his death, gave it into the hands of his closest friend.

In *The Four Zoas,* Blake achieves a synthetic vision of man as a fourfold being. The four elements, or "Mighty ones" as he calls them, are the Four Zoas named Urthona, Urizen, Luvah and Tharmas, and their correspondence in the human being is respectively with the Spirit, Head, Heart and Loins. In their original glory they existed in perfect unity, and in the person of one man, Albion, gave a complete image of the "Universal Man" whom Blake identifies with God. But in creation (that "act of mercy" which permitted division for the sake of conscious identity) each of the Four Zoas in turn divides, projecting its spirit into a material form, or "emanation," with which it afterwards contends in "the torments of love and jealousy."

Night I narrates the division, or materialization, of the Loins: Night II, the division of the Heart: Night III, the division of the Mind: Night IV, the division of the Spirit. In Night V, Ore, symbolizing Sex Instinct, is born of the divided Spirit and its Emanation. And now the fall is complete. Each of the Four Zoas having divided, or fallen, the Spiritual Man is dead.

The whole of this history takes place before the Creation as narrated in the Book of Genesis, for of the man who is the subject of the story we read in *The Last Judgment:* "He is Albion our ancestor, patriarch of the Atlantic Continent, whose history preceded that of the Hebrews, and in whose sleep, or chaos, creation began." Again in the *Descriptive Catalogue* speaking of the three distinctive types of man, the Strong, the Beautiful, and the Ugly, Blake says: "They were originally one man who was fourfold. He was self-divided and his real humanity slain on the stems of generation, and the form of the fourth was like the Son of God. How he became divided is a subject of great sublimity and pathos. The artist has written it under inspiration and will, if God please, publish it; it is voluminous and contains the ancient history of Britain and the world of Satan and of Adam."

In Night VI, the Mind, attempting to think order into chaos, enters the realm of the Spirit and tries to enmesh the fallen world in the web of its reasonable religion. In Night VII, the Fall, according to Genesis, takes place. In Night VIII, Evil becomes materialized and the Crucifixion results. Night IX is devoted to the Last Judgment when Urizen, Luvah, and Tharmas are again united with their Emanations in the inverse order from that in which they were divided: Ore is self-consumed, and the spiritual man, Albion, is raised from the dead.

With the macrocosmic significance of this marvelous epic of the soul of man we are not now concerned, but only with the weight and emphasis it places upon the materialization of instinct.

This we have seen takes place after the fall of the Zoas and is its inevitable result. Whether Instinct is to be regarded as good or evil depends entirely upon the standpoint. In *The Marriage of Heaven and Hell* Instinct appears as the redeemer of the individual. In the *Four Zoas* the ascendency of Instinct is the soul's tragedy. But there is no inconsistency in this. Man's separation from the Divine Essence is at once a tragedy and a triumph, a fall and the beginning of a new creation. Complete incarnation is essential to individuality, yet this incarnation involves separation from God, death and descent into Hell.

The psychological moment of the whole drama is that in which

> Luvah seiz'd the Horses of Light and rose into the Chariot of Day.

In these words, Blake symbolizes the assumption by the emotional powers of the function of the spiritual intelligence. The moment is further described when Urizen in his lamentation cries:

> O did I keep the horses of the day in silver pastures!
> O I refus'd the lord of day the horses of his prince!
> did I close my treasuries with roofs of solid stone,
> And darken all my Palace walls with envyings and hate!

"The horses of the day" are the intellectual powers of the spirit, and "silver pastures" are highly suggestive of the places where human instinct satisfies its hunger indolently. Again, speaking of Luvah, he says:

> Because thou gavest Urizen the wine of the Almighty
> For Steeds of Light, that they might run in thy golden chariot of pride—
> I gave to thee the Steeds, I pour'd the stolen wine,
> And drunken with the immortal draught, fell from my throne sublime.

We know that "wine" is a symbol of emotion: that "Steeds of Light" are spiritual intelligences: that Lucifer fell from heaven through pride. It is easy to see what has happened. Intelligence has been bartered for emotion.

> One dread morn of gory blood
> The manhood was divided; for the gentle passions, making way
> Thro' the infinite labyrinths of the heart and thro' the nostrils issuing
> In odorous stupefaction, stood before the Eyes of Man
> A female bright.

The emotional powers overriding the intelligence, and the intelligence disobedient to the heavenly vision, the mind has become sex-obsessed and mistaken for reality that which is essentially only a means of expression.

Primarily, that is the meaning of *Vala*. Vala herself is Nature—God's means of expression—given identity: she is the maternal or female principle given the finality which alone belongs to God. A matriarchal religion was to Blake the abomination of desolation, for he regarded it as the worship of generation and the enthronement of sex.

> When the Male and Female
> Appropriate Individuality, they become an Eternal Death:
> Hermaphroditic worshippers of a God of cruelty and law.

Not sex, which Blake regarded as a beautiful gift of the Divine Mercy, but the conception of sex as having spiritual identity, was Blake's idea of the fall. The dominance of Sex over Love is, in Blake's symbolism, Luvah become Orc.

Until we perceive that "All Things exist in the Human Imagination" we live at the mercy of unregenerate Instinct, "continually building, continually decaying, because of Love and Jealousy." In dismay we attempt to govern our lives by Reason; but Reason is pitiably insufficient because Instinct lies outside the governance of Reason and will not obey its dictates, legislate as we may. "Love does not know what conscience is," so Love beneath the dictates of Reason creates the permanent image of Sex, which it alternately worships and abhors. Sex thus becomes an absolute, and we are compelled to think in terms of license and repression. We speak of "loving a woman for her womanliness." It is phallic worship. We speak of "the psychology of sex." It is madness; for psychology is the science of the soul, and how can that which is but a means of intercourse be said to have a soul?

But Imagination reveals spiritual form. In our imagination we love a woman for what she is, and while Imagination presents us with a clear and vivid image of unique form, the profoundest reason that ever existed could not give that form a reasonable definition. And as with what is most obvious, so with all things: all things are seen in their eternal reality in the Imagination which places all in proportion. Passion is contained, guided and glorified by the Imagination: Sex is perceived as a sublime concession to lone individuality, a divinely-organized means of atonement, a foretaste of eternal joy, a servant "to the infinite and Eternal of the Human form."

Without the Divine Imagination there must be moral law and condemnation; for what cannot be controlled by love must be subdued by fear. If we have a philosophy of life which exiles the emotions to the region of the untamable, then all that is outside the pale must exist under our tacit condemnation. Instinct is too big and too strong to be controlled by anything but the Imagination. It invades our reasonable enclosure and declares its dominance, crying that Sex has dominion from the cradle to the grave. From the standpoint of materialism, so it is. Life under the guidance of a purely reasonable philosophy is precisely the continuous sex-horror which psychoanalysis shows it to be. "Who shall deliver me from this body of death?" Ultimately, only an imaginative conception of life can save Reason itself.

Blake strove for synthetic life. He inveighed against the materialism which contracts the senses until an acute and suffering localized sensibility displaces an ever-expanding universal joy:

> For the Sanctuary of Eden is in the Camp, in the Outline,
> In the Circumference, and every Minute Particular is Holy:
> Embraces are Comingling's from the Head even to the Feet,
> And not a pompous High Priest entering by a Secret Place.

He neither rejected matter in vague aspiration for immaterial existence, nor worshipped it by dire compulsion, becoming its servant in hateful slavery. He found the Divine Imagination all-encompassing. He saw the world in an actual grain of sand and eternity in the disparate unity of an hour. Nothing was rejected, nothing condemned, nothing cast out; for the whole was contained in the Imagination, and every minute particular seen in divine proportion to have its divinely appointed place.

Man must have an absolute. "The fool hath said in his heart, 'There is no God'." But the bigger fool has said in his mind, 'God is not in *all* his works but is the inhabitant of the eternal invisible void.' Seeing God is living. Seeing oneself and watching the amusing or baleful interplay of one's undirected actions is dying by inches. Man perishes without vision. Blake found that God was to be seen most clearly with the eyes of imagination in the face of man. And there he discovered that the Imagination, perceiving true form, was not distracted by disguise, by disease, by falsity, by denial, or any of the negations which lay hold of the soul that is not filled with the love of God: he found that in Imagination, love was the vision of God. Therefore, he besought his fellow men, with tears of love and cries of longing, to cease from the everlasting misery of executing judgment upon one another, and to look again and see in each human form The Divine Image, even Jesus, the true identity of every man.

10
Forgiveness of Sins

Though Blake probably knew nothing about ultra-violet rays, he certainly ought to be made the patron saint of the societies that want to open our eyes and strip our bodies to the sun's light; for on this side idolatry he worshipped the sun. In the *Descriptive Catalogue* he extols "the flush of health in flesh exposed to the open air," and continues, "as to the modern man, stripped from his load of clothing, he is like a dead corpse." But Blake's respect for the sun went far beyond that: he gave the sun spiritual potency and made it the medium of divine as well as physical power, and so thoroughly deserves canonization. Then the old story about William and Catherine playing Adam and Eve in their garden might gain new, and this time respectful credence, and so in time the picture of them, appropriately unclad, be made the subject of a very pretty crest, worthy to compare with the figure of St. George himself.

In the Seventh Night of *The Four Zoos* it is reported of the inhabitants of Eternity that, when Albion fainted upon the bosom of Vala, "the lily of the desert, melting in high noon," "they saw him dark." That is a very pregnant phrase. Blake took his symbolism of light and darkness straight from the Revelation of St. John, which said of the new Jerusalem "the city had no need of the Sun, neither of the Moon, to shine in it: for the glory of God did lighten it, and the Lamb is the light thereof . . . . And the gates of it shall not be shut at all by day: for there shall be no night there."

Thus the sun became the medium of spiritual life, as we have seen in "The Little Black Boy"; and the moon, which can be gazed upon and has objective beauty to human eyes, yet has no light of her own save what she borrows from the sun, became an apt symbol of the human love which lights man through the darkness of the night of mortality.

Three worlds there were which man in this life inhabited according to his spiritual enlightenment: the world of divine love called Eternity, on earth illumined by the Sun: the world of human love called Beulah, lit by the Moon; and the loveless world of Ulro, or darkness; and with superb understanding and humanity Blake showed that the way out of Ulro to Eternity lay through the moony night of Beulah.

In the "Introduction" to the *Songs of Experience* the Holy Word that walked among the ancient trees, weeping in the evening dew (the Lord God walking in the garden in the cool of the day) calls to the soul to "Arise from out the dewy grass," for "Night is worn and the morn rises from the slumberous mass." That visionary jewel, the little poem "Morning," which in a couple of stanzas epitomizes Blake's whole purpose, tells of the soul cleaving its way through the gates of night to meet the sun. And the journey taken, both in *The Four Zoas* and *Jerusalem,* begins at twilight, is continued through the deepening night and ends with the break of day.

This symbolism was so obvious and simple that it naturally extended itself to man. On one occasion, when Blake wanted to symbolize his own happiness, he described himself as "standing in the porches of the sun," for to be in such a place was to become a prism of light. To him all things became translucent as they were expressions of truth; their spiritual substance offering no impediment to the light, they did not cast a shadow. On the other hand, as things resisted the light and thus became materialized, they began to cast shadows; and when this resistance was permanent, the shadow assumed entity and became error. Satan himself gains identity by such a process of resistance and is described as "the limit of opaqueness." But though Blake saw a limit to opaqueness, with a sublime perception that outfaces all logic and meets with an immediate response in the understanding heart, he saw no limit to translucence. When man becomes as God, man becomes infinite in clarity.

As with light and darkness, so with expansion and contraction. Blake, the arch-enemy of materialism, believed that spiritual man was not the progeny of an anthropoid ape, but a descendant of divine beings whose senses were capable of infinite expansion and contraction at will. He regarded the "Worm a fathom long" that man had apparently (but only apparently) become, as the result of contraction through fear and unbelief. For he knew through his own senses, limited as they were, that through their use he had grown from a helpless infant to a man of full stature, and he understood, as an adult, how he could experience expansion and refinement of his senses by their imaginative exercise. So his faith in man's true genealogy had the warrant of all the logic he required. But when Albion became "dark," mistaking material form for spiritual form, he also became contracted and this contraction goes on as the separation of his essential self from the Divine Essence continues, till, by the time his sickness approaches spiritual death, he flies

> indignant, revengeful, covering
> His face and bosom with petrific hardness, and his hands
> And feet, lest any should enter his bosom and embrace
> His hidden heart.

He hides it "as with iron and steel, dark and opaque."

This limitation continues until Albion reaches the Limit of Contraction, which is the natural man, Adam. But again, though there is a limit of contraction, "there is no limit of expansion in the bosom of man forever from Eternity to Eternity." And when Love, the Breath Divine, at last wakes Albion from his sleep of death and he sees the Divine Image in the face of his brother Los, not only does he become translucent, but he is actually identified with the means whereby the eternal day breaks, while his expansion is such that he becomes imaginatively the habitation of every created thing.

An equally apt and poetic symbol to those of light and darkness, expansion and contraction, Blake found in the idea of the skeleton of the human body and the living man. On what was originally the third sheet of the MS. *Vala* (the lower half of the page is here reproduced), Blake drew a grisly picture of a skeleton man laying bare the form of a siren-faced woman. The skeleton man is obviously Albion and the woman, Vala, who in her spiritual significance becomes Rahab the Harlot. Albion has become a specter, which is to say he has lost all his human attributes, his warm breathing flesh, his hot life's blood, and his nervous sensibilities. He retains, however, most interestingly, the flesh covering to his face and skull, showing that his mind is animate and that he functions now, not with the harmonious unity of a living form, and not with the responsive action of a sentient being, but as an animated brain, coldly curious of sensation. Such an illustration fully explains what Blake means when he says, "The Specter is, in every man, insane and most deform'd." The Spectre is the dehumanized man, and Blake's amazing consistence is realized when we reflect that the Specter exhibits its inhumanity by the loss of *physical* attributes. The Spectre is devoid of those means of sense which, in *The Marriage of Heaven and Hell,* we remember Blake described as "the chief inlets of soul in this age." Man becomes a specter when his feelings are in his brain. By the negation of sensuous attributes common to every living thing, he becomes incapable of communication between himself and the spiritual world.

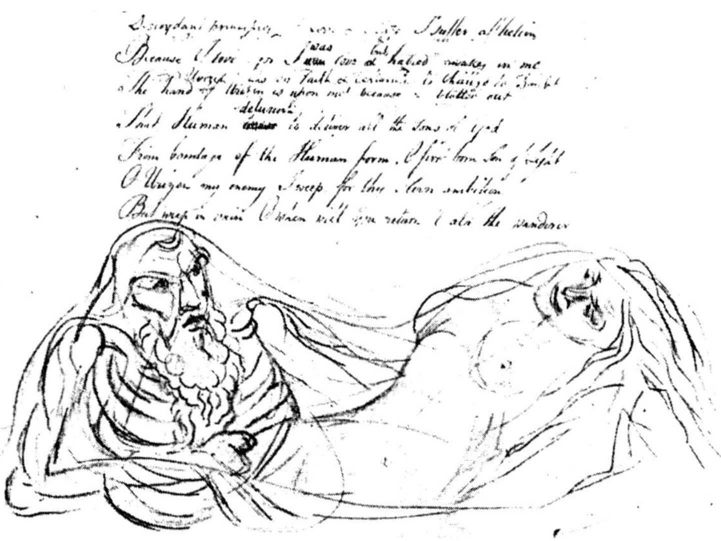

Pencil Sketch from "Vala, or The Four Zoas"

The Spectre is a male creature because man as male is dominantly a creature of intellect, and woman as female is dominantly a creature of instinct. And here perhaps a word of warning to casual readers of Blake who hold feminist or anti-feminist opinions will not be out of place.

Blake regarded sex as a garment which individuals chose at birth and discarded at death. These garments are

> woven with care
> Lest the sexual garments sweet
> Should grow a devouring winding-sheet.

They are for a period, to preserve the body in the grave of mortality and their use is completed before mortal life is finished. But "The Sexual is Threefold, the Human is Fourfold"; "Humanity is far above sexual organization"; for every man and every woman has, by the inherent right of Divine Mercy, a human form divine which is beyond sex and is to be clearly distinguished from the mere garment which the soul chooses to wear during its mortal pilgrimage. The idea, therefore, that any human being could be identified by, much less confined to, sex function is utterly foreign to Blake, as a right reading of *Visions of the Daughters of Albion* ought to convince us.

Contrasted with the Specter is the Emanation or life-giving portion of the spiritual man. The dictionary defines emanation as "person or thing proceeding from the Divine Essence," and that is exactly how Blake used the word. The human soul was the emanation of God. Blake saw everything as proceeding from the Divine Essence and possessing the power of again raying out beams from the divine source. His emanations are light giving radiations from the divine sun: they are the outward-shining light without which the body becomes dark, the means of translucence without which the body becomes opaque. They are the soul's perceptive means of apprehension without which it becomes, in Meredith's phrase, "inlay only thrilling shrewd."

But, as we have seen in the instance of Albion, the emanation is also the sensuous and instinctive part of the man. Therefore the emanation is to the individual as the wife to the husband. And since Blake transfigured Milton's idea of the sexes and said that the female lives from the light of the male, it is always severance from spiritual life which precedes the separation of the emanation from the body. When that life is regained, reunion takes place: but so long as there is separation, the struggle for dominance goes on, the dependent part, or emanation, developing, for the purposes of contention, a will of its own which is described as "the female will."

Everyone is conscious of his own specter and emanation. I believe in the evil eye, and I shudder to think of the power my own evil eye can exert. It can darken the atmosphere of a room and send forth venomous spirits of discord that wound the spirits of love in their wings. It can blight the lives of children and hang a curtain between the sun's rays and innocence. It can murder the Holy One without a glance. But mercifully, I also know of eyes that are prisms of divine light, eyes "open to joy and to delight wherever beauty appears," eyes that are attractive to innocence and without defense to love, eyes that can sometimes look upon corruption with insight.

The whole of our critical faculty is the Specter's realm. The whole of our creative activity depends upon the Emanation. They are interdependent; for as the body cannot stand without its bony structure, so, apart from form, thought is impossible, and as the body without its organs is dead, so criticism without creation is mere intellectual anatomy.

The Spectre is Mr. Worldly Wiseman, the Snowing cynic, the rapacious destructive power, the self-exhibitive self, the self-secretive self, the hawk, the fox, the shark, the artist as artiste. The Emanation is the delighted mind, the pitiful eye, the generous heart, the open countenance, the compassionate bowels, the long-suffering affections. It is love itself. But love divided from imagination Blake describes as "an eternal death." So when the emanation, divided from its male counterpart, strives for dominion overall, the light of the soul is eclipsed and instinct stalks abroad like a wild beast craving to put all into its maw. The female will rear its altars in the "infernal Grove" and love becomes a rite with ceremonies that entail in its final act the devouring of its own offspring.

Blake suffered from the tyranny of his own specter. I know of no more moving picture in all literature than that presented in the opening passages of *Jerusalem,* where the frustrated poet, despised by his friends, rejected by the public, dogged by poverty, hidden in obscurity, wrestles with the demon of doubt and detraction (Blake's own critical mind) that would dissuade him from the mighty task he had conceived:

To open the Eternal Worlds, to open the immortal Eyes
Of Man inwards into the Worlds of Thought: into Eternity
Ever expanding in the Bosom of God, the Human
Imagination.

There was not a single argument that prudence or personal dignity could advance in favour of such an enterprise at such a time. There were a thousand perfectly eligible reasons why he should abandon it. How those reasons must have pleaded for his regard! But Blake was the Job of his age. His integrity nothing could shake. So, with superhuman will, he forces the demon of doubt to beat alternate strokes on the anvil of creation. It is Eternity and Time beating out the hours and minutes of human existence; but it is also a titanic spirit struggling with his own destructive self-criticism till criticism is made the servant of creation. It is the phoenix rising from the ashes.

Spectre and Emanation, Translucence and Opacity, Expansion and Contraction—these are Blake's means of regarding man in his inevitably dual state.

So long as life lasts, instinct and imagination war within him. Once separated from the Divine Essence and endowed with the power of instinct, man becomes master of his own house, a unique, distinguishable, personal identity, severed from God, and, in a human body, separate and distinct from every other human being. Through instinct he reaches the limit of contraction, he becomes the natural man, and so long as he remains contracted into a mortal body he remains, in measure, a creature of instinct seeking his own, to the annihilation of all the world besides, if need be.

Yet consciousness endows him with the power of Imagination. To what purpose?

We answer that question according to the power of Imagination within us. Blake believed the ultimate purpose of Imagination was to create in us "the Spirit of Jesus" which he described as "continual forgiveness of sin."

Forgiveness of Sin! It is a common phrase, glib upon the lips of the professing Church.

I "forgive and forget/I call it forgiveness when I omit the actual execution of my revenge. I forgive by relegating the subject of my forgiveness to a rank of inferiority far below my magnanimous self. Or I cover myself with a cloak of sentimental deceit: a complete robe of self-righteousness. This I call "a forgiving spirit/In it I act the liar to those who have offended me, by a show of manners contradicted by every impulse of my heart. Or, darker still, I climb into the seat of the spiritual coroner and hold an intellectual inquest on the body of him who has done me harm. Without undue emotion I hear the evidence: with Christian charity I bring in the verdict of temporary insanity. So far as I am concerned, the man is dead. I have rounded his life with a statement of his faults and virtues which, for truth and accuracy, none could gainsay. Then, out of my consummate understanding of his case, I "forgive/It is only reasonable.

Or I forgive conditionally. I want to forgive after the manner of monarchs sparing the lives of helpless captives. I have heard that with God 'repentance precedes forgiveness; so I apply the doctrine to man. Avowed repentance is only required of children, who must "say they are sorry'; of adults I expect the acts of contrition. And this I can justify most reasonably; for, after all, surely he who has done the wrong should admit it? Truth demands it, and all I want is the truth. Would it not be hypocritical to ignore the demand of truth? Should I not actively encourage him to repeat the offence whom I forgive even before he realizes what he has done ? And is there even commonsense, let alone morality, in tacitly encouraging a friend to continue in ignorant error? Surely any sort of unconditional forgiveness would destroy all sense of values and bring one who practised it to the state of the flabby sentimentalist who does not know an enemy from a friend?

Great honour has conditional forgiveness. It is a bulwark of the Church. It is divine in the eyes of the Law. It commends itself to every reasonable man as the limit of human charity. That a man, having suffered injury, should hold himself in readiness to forgive on the least indication of the offender's contrition—what more could be asked? And if that is indeed the limit, anything else must be insane. How can I forgive a man before I know whether he wants to be forgiven?

Thus my highest conception of forgiveness appears as a contract of which the offender shall pay the stamp and lawyer's fee. There does not seem to be anything particularly divine about it. Indeed it looks unmistakably like self-justification.

The Spirit of Satan is continual self-justification.

Blake wrote his longest and greatest book simply to explain what he understood by the forgiveness of sin. That is the theme of *Jerusalem*. Ultimately it is about nothing else.

Jerusalem was his synonym for spiritual liberty. How was spiritual liberty to be achieved? How could man, the instinctive unit, be transformed into the likeness of God, the imaginative reality? How could instinct and imagination become synthetic? Could the antagonistic and contrary principles in man be reconciled? And if so, where and how?

Imagination teaches us that the cause of true love is recognition of identity. Why do I love my friend? Truly I cannot tell you. That he exists, separate and distinct from all other men, this I know; yet he shares this singularity with all. If I analyse him and describe his virtues in detail, am I any nearer the secret? On the contrary, I have only broken up a living unity into incoherent and inanimate parts. I do not know my friend as a collection of qualities. If I attempt a definition by describing the effects he has in me, still I get no further, for I only confuse the clear and vivid image I have of him with my own amiable or faulty reactions. No, I love a person, not an effect.

Specter and Emanation he has. His Specter I fear and dread. His Emanation I know by its heart-searching beauty: by its effect in me, and mine in him, we are friends. But he is not his emanation or his specter. There is a unity beyond which I cannot define: a unity that is God-like, and yet not God: the unity of a man, yet not of a mortal form.

And this that I know quite clearly for my friend is truly more glorious than I can describe. Only in poems, better than I can write, could I show him to you. My friend does not know his own potentialities. He does not know his intrinsic surpassing beauty. But I know and exist to reveal it to him in myself as in a mirror. His greatness he does not know. He is capable of infinite expansion—of taking the whole world to his heart—of speaking words that angels would leave heaven to hear. I tell you I have seen God in the eyes of my friend. In essence he is the express image of the Father. In identity he is one with the son.

And I sin against him, or he against me (what does it matter?) And we hate each other with a ferocity you could scarce believe. He crystallizes into the image of all I most detest. He becomes for me the very limit of opacity. His sin cries to heaven for vengeance, and something in me makes me aware in terror that I should like to be the instrument of heaven.

I hate and hate and cannot forgive; for to do this would be to extenuate what I regard as a blasphemy against his true self. It is because I love that true self that I am compelled to hate this falsity.

What shall I do? I am utterly divided by love and hate and only my hatred can find expression. I would give all I have to show him his error. What more could a man do for his friend? Yet are avails nothing: absolutely nothing.

I dig myself up by the roots. At least I can find my own error. But no: all coheres. There is nothing to be done. I can only wait and hope: mind my own business and see to it that I am not a virtuous hypocrite. And this is not so easy; for loathsome self-justification seems to be turning me, day by day, more and more, into this virtuous hypocrite. In every relationship frankness and honesty seem to be infected.

Here is new cause for hatred. I now begin to hate him for his ill effects in me.

And all the while, deep down, under all, there is unrest.

I can at least face this. And when I do, I find that this unrest would not be stilled though God himself should vindicate my cause.

> My Emanation far within
> Weeps incessantly for my sin.

What is my sin? I cannot find it. I swear that I desire nothing but the truth and would welcome it though it should slay me. But the assertion, oft-repeated, does not silence this weeping.

I cannot pretend to crimes that were not mine, though for the sake of peace I am even tempted to this madness.

What shall I do? The ache of unrest goes on.

Who is this weeping angel?

> The Divine Vision still was seen:
> Still was the Human Form Divine:

Weeping in weak and mortal clay,
O Jesus, still the Form was thine.

Blake said, "He who waits to be righteous before he enters into the Saviour's Kingdom, the Divine Body, will never enter there."

Each Man is in his Spectre's power
Until the arrival of that hour
When his Humanity awake
And cast his Spectre into the Lake.

And what is "his Humanity"? Blake identifies man's humanity with the Divine Imagination.

So long as I am content to act as an instinctive being insisting upon my individual identity, its rights and the respect due to it as such, I am putting up an invulnerable barrier between myself and my friend. But perchance I lose sight of myself for a moment, and then what do I see?

A third figure between him and me—the light now become the life—standing in the place where we used to meet, now suffering the torments of our love and jealousy.

And O, thou Lamb of God, whom I
Slew in my dark self-righteous pride,
Art thou return'd to Albion's Land,
And is Jerusalem thy Bride?

Come to my arms and never more
Depart, but dwell forever here:
Create my Spirit to thy Love,
Subdue my Spectre to thy Fear.

Spectre of Albion warlike Fiend!
In clouds of blood and ruin roll'd,
I here reclaim thee as my own,
My Selfhood, Satan, arm'd in gold.

Without vision the forgiveness of sin is an impossibility. The forgiveness of sin is a continual death in the Divine Image.

"How oft shall my brother sin against me?"

Only by identification of my friend with the Divine Image can I forgive him: all else is mere hypocrisy. But when I see him as he is, then I know who he is, and who I am. What do I care for right or wrong when we are, as Blake says, "wholly One in

Jesus our Lord." Henceforth, in us at least, "Heaven, Earth and Hell shall live in harmony."

Job's Sacrifice